GIANT
-IN-
CHAINS

The author at the Great Wall

GIANT -IN- CHAINS

CHINA
TODAY & TOMORROW

JOHN WARWICK MONTGOMERY

Giant in Chains

© 2021 New Reformation Publications

All rights reserved. No part of this publication may be reproduced, distributed, or transmitted in any form or by any means, including photocopying, recording, or other electronic or mechanical methods, without the prior written permission of the publisher, except in the case of brief quotations embodied in critical reviews and certain other noncommercial uses permitted by copyright law. For permission requests, write to the publisher at the address below.

All scripture quotations are taken from the King James Version.

Published by:
1517 Publishing
PO Box 54032
Irvine, CA 92619-4032

Publisher's Cataloging-In-Publication Data
(Prepared by The Donohue Group, Inc.)

Names: Montgomery, John Warwick, author.
Title: Giant in chains : China today and tomorrow / John Warwick Montgomery.
Description: Second, revised edition. | Irvine, CA : 1517 Publishing, [2021]
   | Originally published: Milton Keynes, England : Word Publishing, ©1994.
   | Includes bibliographical references and index.
Identifiers: ISBN 9781948969666 (paperback) | ISBN 9781948969673 (ebook)
Subjects: LCSH: China—History—1949- | China—Religion. | Christianity—
   China. | Religion and politics—China.
Classification: LCC DS779.215 .M66 2021 (print) | LCC DS779.215 (ebook)
   | DDC 951.05—dc23

Printed in the United States of America

Cover art by Brenton Clarke Little

For

CAROL

Flowers exhale thin mist when daylight fades away;
The sleepless feel sad to see the moon shed silken ray.
My harp on phoenix-holder has just become mute,
I'll try to play upon lovebird strings of my lute.
    My song's a message.

Her face is seen in flower and her dress in cloud,
    A beauty
    caressed by vernal breeze.
If not a fairy queen from Jade-Green Mountains proud
    She's Goddess of the Moon in Crystal Hall one sees.

                          Li Po (701–762)

CONTENTS

By Way of Introduction ... ix

Introduction to the
   Second English Edition ... xi

Acknowledgements ... xiii

PART 1. POLITICS AND RELIGION

Chapter 1.   The June Explosion ... 3

Chapter 2.   How the World Reacted:
                  Hong Kong ... 23

Chapter 3.   Marxism in China ... 65

Chapter 4.   China's Religious Heritage ... 93

Chapter 5.   The Church in China:
                  Is There a Gospel Answer? ... 137

PART 2. ESSAYS FOR CONTEMPORARY CHRISTIAN SINOPHILES (AND FOR CYNICAL RELIGIOUS LIBERALS AND PAGANS)

Why You Should Not
   Buy Into Confucianism ... 181

The Gospel Accounts: Historical Fact or Narrative Fiction?	189
Why Not Regard the Gospel Narratives as Fictional Constructs?	193
Why Two Excellent Nineteenth-Century Scholars Rejected Biblical Truth	199
Coronavirus	207
Are Coronavirus Restrictions Illegal?	213
Punishment and Works-Righteousness	217
Notes	219
The Author	239
Index of Names	241

BY WAY OF
INTRODUCTION

*I*t is said that the devil meets his victim at a crossroad. The events of June 1989, in Beijing were a crossroad in the history of modern China. The leadership of the most populous country in the world thereby gave notice that China would pursue its totalitarian and anti-democratic route whatever the consequences.

In the months that followed, one Eastern European country after the other chose a diametrically opposite path. With hardline pressure from the Soviet Union vastly reduced through Gorbachev's philosophy of *glasnost*, Eastern Europe has turned its back on monolithic Marxism.

Why this staggering contrast between China and the rest of the Marxist world? What can explain the particular choice made by China at its unique crossroad?

I was privileged to be in Beijing during the fateful days in which so many lost their lives for ideals which their leadership opposed. This book is an attempt to understand the root causes of what occurred and to determine what solutions may exist for China in the '90s.

To arrive at a meaningful analysis of today's China, one must not only see the situation at firsthand: one must also penetrate to the depth-level of the Chinese mind. Arnold Toynbee quite rightly argued that civilisations and religions interlock, and that one cannot comprehend a culture without understanding its ways of viewing ultimate religious reality.

The present volume does not shrink from such analysis. We shall look carefully at the effects of the traditional religions of China on its approach to the modern world, and examine in depth the most influential contemporary 'religion' of China, that of orthodox Marxism. Some remarkable insights will surface in the course of our comparative analysis, and it will be difficult for the reader any longer to sustain the popular viewpoint that 'it does not matter what you believe as long as you are sincere'.

Indeed, this book should bring its reader to the conviction that both for China and for the individual (whether of the East or of the West), the only way to societal health is the reorientation of life on the basis of ultimate values that are truly ultimate.

John Warwick Montgomery

Strasbourg, France
June 1990
Pentecost
The Anniversary of the Massacre

INTRODUCTION TO THE SECOND ENGLISH EDITION

*T*he thirtieth anniversary of the Tiananmen Square atrocity has just gone by—ignored (to be sure) by the Chinese government but well remembered in the Western democracies.

What has occurred since 1989? It should come as no surprise that, under its present dictatorial, Marxist regime, civil liberties continue to be stifled whilst economic progress continues.

The current leadership has, for example, very recently announced a policy under which religions in China are called upon to revise or reinterpret their sacred writings to conform to Communist ideals.[1] And the central government's efforts to de-democratise Hong Kong have resulted in significant quasi–Tiananmen Square protests in that Westernised, anomalous city. *Plus ça change plus c'est la même chose.*

---

1. The Chinese government's new, official biblical 'translation' has not yet appeared, but journalist Cameron Hilditch has reported that a government-published high school textbook now includes the following—utterly non-textual and heretical—addition to the story in John 8 of the woman taken in adultery: 'When the crowd disappeared, Jesus stoned the sinner to death saying, I too am a sinner. But if the law could only be executed by men without blemish, the law would be dead.' Hilditch, 'China's Communist Christ', *National Review*, 1 October 2020.

Western Christians need to be sensitised to the most populous country in the world. This new edition of *China in Chains* contains seven essays, largely apologetical in character, with a Chinese twist. They follow in part from the author's labours in obtaining a diploma in basic Chinese language studies. He trusts that readers in the East and West will enjoy and benefit from them.

John Warwick Montgomery

Strasbourg, France
3 June 2020

ACKNOWLEDGEMENTS

*M*y deep appreciation to the authors and publishers of copyrighted materials quoted herein. Every effort has been made to identify sources by way of bibliographical notes; any inadvertent omissions brought to the Author's attention will be rectified in subsequent printings.

OPINIONS EXPRESSED IN THIS BOOK ARE SOLELY THE AUTHOR'S. They should under no circumstances be attributed to mainland Chinese interviewed, mentioned, or photographed.

Thanks to the intrepid group who accompanied my wife and me on the pilgrimage to China which gave rise to this book. After all their anxieties, they deserve to be immortalised by being listed here!

Elsie H. Daniell	Chatham, N.J.
Dr. Robert O. and Mrs Connie Hansen	Prospect Heights, Il.
Dr. Stephanie Hutchinson	Los Angeles, Ca.
Jack W. and Frances F. Knauf	Fairfax, Va.
John E. and Erleen Martin	Tucson, Az.
Arthur E. Prosser	Wilmington, N.C.
Richard A. Schaeffer	Richardson, Tx.
Tammy Spitler	Cape Girardeau, Mo.
Lorena F. Stiles	McLean, Va.
Harold and Barbara Tonnesen	Barrington, Il.

PART ONE

POLITICS AND RELIGION

CHAPTER ONE

THE JUNE EXPLOSION

On June 3-4, 1989, what had begun as massive but peaceful political protest in Tiananmen Square, Beijing, became a bloodbath. Government efforts to control and repress the news of what was occurring were doomed to fail; there was no way to cut off instantaneous electronic communication. Thus, on June 6, telefax machines throughout Tokyo and in many other parts of the world received the following *cri de coeur*.

—TOP URGENCY—

CHINESE COMMUNISTS ARE PROCEEDING BRUTAL SLAUGHTERING. THEIR TROOPS GO ON SHOOTING MADLY AT THOUSANDS OF INNOCENT PEOPLE WITH MACHINE GUNS & OTHER WEAPONS. OVER 7,000 PEOPLE WERE KILLED INCLUDING MAINLY STUDENTS, THE GENERAL PUBLIC, THE OLD AND SOME WOMEN, EVEN CHILDREN! THE NUMBER OF THE CORPSES THAT PILING UP IN BEIJING IS STILL INCREASING RAPIDLY NOW.

PLEASE SAVE THE PEOPLE IN CHINA! PLEASE!! PLEASE, WHATEVER MEANS! WE URGE AND BEG YOU! PLEASE! DON'T CONSIDER IT TO BE NONE OF YOUR BUSINESS. PLEASE![1]

All civilised peoples need to make this tragedy 'their business'. Let us do so by surveying the events leading up to and immediately following the Tiananmen slaughter. A straightforward chronology will assist as a starting-point; we shall then offer personal insights on the basis of eyewitness testimony.

A Chronology of Tragedy

In an appendix to their valuable composite work, *Massacre in Beijing*, the editors of *Time* magazine list key political events occurring in China from 1972 to 1989. The concluding portion of that chronology, from 15 April to the end of July, 1989, will assist greatly in situating ourselves to analyse what occurred and, more importantly, why it occurred.[2]

April 15	Former C.C.P. General Secretary Hu Yaobang dies at 74.
April 16	Thousands of students march to Tiananmen Square to mourn Hu's death.
April 21–22	Defying government orders forbidding demonstrations during the official memorial ceremonies held for Hu in the Great Hall of the People, up to 100,000 people join the students at Tiananmen Square, demanding freedom and democracy.
April 26	The *People's Daily* publishes a controversial editorial denouncing student demonstrators as a 'small bunch of troublemakers' and threatening a government crackdown.
April 29	After the government refuses to meet with student leaders, demonstrations are held in Beijing, Shanghai, Nanjing and other major cities, demanding democracy and freedom of the press.
May 4	A massive march commemorates the seventieth anniversary of a historic student protest movement and coincides with an Asian Development Bank meeting in Beijing.

May 13	In Tiananmen Square, 3,000 students begin a hunger strike.
May 14	At a secret Politburo meeting, Zhao Ziyang's moderate line in handling the student demonstrations is reportedly adopted. The policy calls for a direct dialogue with student leaders and limited measures to implement democracy within the Party.
May 15	Soviet President Mikhail Gorbachev arrives in Beijing for the first Sino-Soviet summit since 1959. Because of the hunger strike and continuing demonstrations, the welcoming ceremony is held at the Beijing airport instead of Tiananmen Square.
May 18	More than 1 million people take to-the streets in Beijing to support the hunger strikers;
May 19	Zhao Ziyang makes an emotional pre-dawn visit to the hunger strikers, pleading with students to leave the square. Li Peng warns that Beijing's turmoil has spread to other parts of the country and holds a televised meeting with a delegation of students led by Uerkesh Daolet (Wuer Kaixi).
May 20	Martial law is officially declared by Li Peng in 'some parts of Beijing'. Speaking to a selected audience of party leaders, Yang Shankun justifies martial law and the deployment of troops in the capital to 'keep order'.
May 25	Premier Li calls on the troops to 'overcome difficulties and carry out martial law'.
May 27	Some student leaders urge demonstrators to end the occupation of Tiananmen Square, but others escalate their demands for Premier Li to step down.
June 2	Unarmed troops try to enter Tiananmen Square and are pushed back by student demonstrators.
June 3	Armed soldiers begin to move to Tiananmen Square. Clashes between soldiers and civilians break out on the western and southern outskirts of Beijing.
June 4	Troops in armoured personnel carriers and tanks crash through barriers and fire indiscriminately at students and city residents, killing thousands of people.

June 6	Protest leader Liu Xiaobo, later branded by Beijing as the 'black hand' behind the unrest, is arrested while riding a bicycle in Beijing.
June 7	Pro-democracy Astrophysicist Fang Lizhi, his wife Li Shuxian and son Fang Ke take refuge in the U.S. embassy in Beijing.
June 9	Deng Xiaoping, who had not been seen in public since his meeting with Gorbachev on May 16, appears on national television to congratulate the commanders of the martial-law troops.
June 10	The Beijing municipal government announces the arrest of more than 400 people, including students, intellectuals and labour leaders.
June 13	The Public Security Bureau issues arrest warrants for 21 leaders of the Autonomous Students' Union of Beijing Universities, including Wang Dan and Uerkesh Daolet.
June 23–24	Following an enlarged Politburo plenum (June 19–21), the Central Committee meets in Beijing to endorse the crackdown and condemn Zhao Ziyang. Zhao is stripped of all leading posts and replaced as party General Secretary by Shanghai party chief and mayor Jiang Zemin.
June 27	The National People's Congress opens after a nine-day postponement. Chaired by Wan Li, the body endorses the crackdown of the 'counter-revolutionary rebellion' and joins the call for tighter ideological control.
June 30	In a report to the National People's Congress Standing Committee, Beijing Mayor Chen Xitong details criticisms of deposed party chief Zhao Ziyang.
July 29	The *People's Daily* publishes a Politburo decision: to 1. Purge state-controlled companies. 2. Prohibit children of high cadres from engaging in business. 3. Stop the 'special supply' of food to top party leaders. 4. Strictly regulate the use of official automobiles and forbid luxury sedan imports. 5. Prohibit the use of public funds for dinner parties or gifts. 6. Strictly control foreign travel. 7. Investigate cases of corruption, bribery and other crimes.

A Personal Adventure

The bare recounting of events—even remarkable and exciting events—is one thing; personally experiencing them is quite another! During the most crucial two weeks of the Chinese upheaval, from 31 May to 13 June, my wife and I found ourselves in the eye of the storm, able to evaluate the situation on the basis of eyewitness experience.

For more than twenty years, I have made an avocation of organising and conducting at least one annual tour to out-of-the-way places. Following my own explorations on Mount Ararat in eastern Turkey in the early 1970s,[3] I took a group into that forbidden and exceedingly difficult mountainous region. During the 1970s and 1980s, I regularly introduced Americans and western Europeans to the Reformation sites on the other side of the Iron Curtain.[4] In 1987, we were in Fiji when it revolted against the British Crown. In 1989, we went to China—and, as it turned out, entered directly into history!

Our scheduled itinerary underwent only slight modifications even with the disturbances in Beijing and throughout the country. The chief modifications were our remaining in Nanjing several extra days because of the impossibility of getting to Shanghai during the crisis there; and the prolongation of our stay in the People's Republic by a full day owing to the temporary cancellation of air service from Guilin to Hong Kong. Otherwise, virtually everything proceeded on schedule—with the unparalleled opportunity to observe an abortive struggle for liberty.

On arriving in Beijing, one could almost palpably feel the tension: the psychological atmosphere was heavy, like the sky just before a summer electrical storm breaks.

Since April, students had been demonstrating in Tiananmen Square. They had picked this location for very good reason. The Square is the largest public square in the world—880 metres by 500 metres in size and can hold half a million people. There one finds the Chairman Mao Memorial Hall, completed in 1977 after Mao's death to display his embalmed corpse, as Lenin's body is displayed in Red Square, Moscow. (Materialists, lacking a Resurrection, are reduced to such practices!) In the Square one also finds a Monument to the People's Heroes, an obelisk dedicated to martyrs of the revolutionary struggle. There are two museums, the Museum of Chinese History and the Museum of the Chinese Revolution. On the western side of the Square is the Great Hall of the Peoples, the seat of the National People's Congress. One official government publication puts it this way:

> Tiananmen is the symbol of modern China because the May 4th Movement of 1919, which marked the beginning of the new-democratic revolution in China, was launched there. It is also the place where the inauguration of the People's Republic of China was held.[5]

The protesters, in other words, were well aware of the quintessential symbolic value of occupying the Square. Here history—revolutionary history—had been made. Now, they were saying, it could be made again!

For the first two weeks of the April protests, no significant government reaction occurred. It was not until Tuesday night, 25 April, that the Chinese Communist Party met to denounce the student activity. At that point, the Party called for 'a grave political struggle' against the student unrest. Here is the *New York Times* report of the situation at that stage:

> The harshness of the message, which charged that the unrest was a conspiracy to wrest power from the party, immediately prompted fears among students that a crackdown was imminent. Similar wording was

used in warnings that accompanied crackdowns against unrest in 1987 and 1976.

Students at two prominent Beijing universities rallied Tuesday night and vowed to continue their class boycotts, but some students seemed ready to back away from their more aggressive tactics.

The party announcement was read over the evening television news as the first item, and also released by the official New China News Agency. The statement was based on the partial contents of an editorial published today in *People's Daily*, the official newspaper of the Communist Party Central Committee.

'All the comrades of the party and the whole nation must understand clearly,' a solemn television newscaster announced, 'that if we do not resolutely stop this unrest, our state will have no calm days. Our reform and modernization will depend on this struggle, and the future of our state and nation will depend on it.'

The student demonstrations began shortly after the death April 15 of the former Communist Party leader, Hu Yaobang, who had been forced to resign two years ago after an earlier round of student demonstrations.

At their peak late last week, the demonstrations in the center of Beijing attracted more than 100,000 people mourning Hu and urging greater democracy. The demonstrators called for press freedom, the right to demonstrate, punishment of corrupt officials and a reappraisal of Hu's role in history.

Since Hu's funeral ceremony Saturday, the democracy campaign has entered a quieter phase.

More than 1,000 students from the Beijing Institute of Technology marched through the

> capital Tuesday, waving such banners as 'Democracy
> Forever', but in general, students have focused their
> energies on writing posters and organizing an
> indefinite class boycott that seems to be enjoying
> overwhelming support at universities throughout
> the capital.

By the time we arrived in Beijing, a month later, the government had still not taken any concrete action to remove the protesters from the Square, but rumours were becoming more and more ominous that their days were numbered. Troops were supposed to have been brought in to ring the city to make possible a final crackdown. As a result—and because the protest did not seem to be motivating a general strike or general popular uprising—many of the protestors previously occupying the Square had decamped. Those remaining naively believed that since the government had not done anything yet, it would not in fact move against them. This belief was reinforced by the fact that when troops on the outskirts of the city had been ordered into the city, the people themselves took to the streets to block the arteries by which the military could get to the Square. Thus the remaining protesters believed that even if the government was so foolish as to try to crush them, the people would never allow it.

It was at this point, in the forty-eight hours before the 3–4 June holocaust, that we had personal contact with the Square and its students. Our photographs may be the last taken before all was swept away in blood and tragedy. How poignant especially was the glorious 'Goddess of Democracy' (modelled on the French-American Statue of Liberty) which the students raised to symbolise their hopes! It became a particular object of the soldiers' venom when they descended on the Square with tanks and weaponry to clean out the defenceless protesters.

I had been in Paris during the 'Petite Révolution' (the so-called 'jours de mai') of 1968. Though the ideology of the French students had been almost exactly the opposite of the Tiananmen protestors—the former were Maoists and anarchists ('Ni Dieu ni maître!') while the latter were trying to oppose totalitarian Marxism—I was impressed by the parallel naïveté of the two movements. Both idealistically believed that protest for a good cause *must* succeed. They were like the hopeless revolutionaries in Hugo's *Les Misérables*, who saw human nature as basically good and therefore able to triumph over any odds. But original sin is always there—power tends to corrupt, and absolute power corrupts absolutely and Chairman Deng sent in troops from the hinterlands (many of whom did not even speak Chinese) who had no difficulty depersonalising the students and slaughtering them like the revisionist enemies of the state they were supposed to be. The government's total indifference to international law and human rights was also illustrated by marauding army vehicles which drove through the streets, especially in the foreign and diplomatic quarters of the city, firing at random.

On 3 June, we caught what may well have been the last flight out of Beijing for Xian. The doors of the plane were just ready to close when we reached the tarmac. It had been almost impossible to drive from the centre of town to the airport because of the massed demonstrations. Again and again we had to turn the bus around and try another route. My philosophy (it wasn't the driver's!) was that if we waited for traffic to clear we would get permanently bogged down in the sea of people: our only hope was to keep searching for a hole. Finally we found it and were able to get to the airport by a circuitous back road.

On our arrival, Xian presented a much calmer atmosphere than Beijing. The city now constitutes an archeological mecca as a result of the discovery of the remarkable

Terracotta Warriors and Horses of Emperor Qin Shi Huang. These life-size, meticulously crafted troops were buried more than two thousand years ago and only unearthed in 1974. Only a portion have even yet been uncovered in the intervening years of archeological work on the Emperor's mausoleum. We stood in awe at this reminder of the overwhelming impact of the cult of the emperor on Chinese history—a consideration of no trivial significance (as we shall see) for understanding the current miseries of that land.

On Sunday morning we were privileged to attend services at the China Christian Church on New South Street (Pastor Sun's congregation). The building was packed to the rafters and many people stood outside within earshot so as to benefit from the music and the preaching. As we shall note later, there is only one, amalgamated Protestant denomination in China, so ecumenicity has been imposed from above—but in congregations such as this one the result has in no way lessened evangelical fervour. Dynamism and spirituality were apparent on all levels. Particularly valuable was our contact with Tian Jing-fu, regional chairman of the Committee of the Three-Self Movement and its council president; the importance of this much misunderstood movement will be discussed in chapter 5 of our book.

At the Greater Wild Goose Pagoda (Da Yan Ta), originally constructed in 652 and frequently restored or renovated across the centuries, it is customary to climb the seven tiers to obtain (not enlightenment à la Thomass Merton's seven-storey mountain!) but a surpassing view of Xian. This we did, and on the top level I encountered a talkative member of the Chinese Communist Party who had just heard about the repression in Beijing. He condemned the government's actions in no uncertain terms. Indeed, said he, at the general assembly of the Party weeks before, the delegates had overwhelmingly expressed support for the student protesters. Thus the Party leadership had simply ignored its members' wishes and opinions and done whatever they themselves claimed was best for the country. I pointed out that this wasn't the first time in the history of Marxism that this had occurred! My Party member ruefully agreed.

By Monday, word concerning the brutal events that had occurred in Beijing over the weekend began to spread like wildfire in Xian. Parades and demonstrations were everywhere and as yet there was no police or government attempt at an equivalent crackdown in Xian. Again we faced the problem of getting to the airport. With the greatest of difficulty we were able to persuade the protesters that we ourselves favoured their cause. Of course, we had obtained and made sure we wore the now historic 'V' button of the protest movement. Finally, students were willing to remove street barriers for us, permitting our bus to drive partially on the sidewalks and thereby get through the crowds to reach the airport. After our CAAC flight to Nanjing got into the air we learned that the Xian airport had been closed down tight. That made two close shaves in four days!

The rest of our time in China was divided between Nanjing and Guilin, for there was no possibility of reaching Shanghai. We were to have taken the train from Nanjing to Shanghai on Wednesday 7 June, but just hours before we were to depart, passenger train 161 from Beijing to Shanghai ran over peaceful demonstrators near the Shanghai station; as a result, infuriated protestors attacked and burned the train, Nine coaches were destroyed, and all railway traffic between Shanghai and Hangzhou and between Shanghai and Nanjing was suspended.[6] Getting in or out of Shanghai by any means became a virtual impossibility.

In Nanjing we profited by a longer-than-scheduled stay to visit two of the key centres of Christian work in the country: the Nanjing Union Theological Seminary for the training of Protestant clergy, and the Amity Printing Press where a remarkable programme of Bible publishing has recently moved into high gear.

At the Seminary—China's largest—I was privileged to lecture to the students, with the genial assistance of Pastor Bao Jia-quan of the Nanjing office of the China Christian Council who served as my translator. Here Billy Graham had met with the Seminary community a year earlier.[7] The number of students was somewhat reduced owing to the upheaval, but discussion was vigorous. We shall leave to our final chapters in this section a theological analysis of the events of June 1989, but the importance of the Nanjing Seminary warrants attention at this point. Here is the institution's self-description:

> Nanjing Union Theological Seminary is a Protestant-church-related institution offering professional and academic education for the ministry. It also aims to train theological teachers, research workers as well as Christian writers, musicians and artists. Established in 1952 through the union of twelve theological colleges and schools, later united with Yenjing Union Theological Seminary in 1961, it has trained hundreds of Christian workers who are now serving the church in many provinces. After an interruption during the 'cultural revolution' it was reopened in 1981. At present there is an enrollment of over 160, about one-third, being female, average age 23. There are three levels of training; a two-year junior programme plus one year internship, a four-year collegiate programme, both for senior middle school graduates, and a three to four-year seminary programme for university graduates. The Extension Department compiles and publishes a quarterly 'Syllabus' or teach-yourself material, for rural and lay church workers, with a

distribution of about 40,000. Committed to Biblical truths and preserving the historical Christian faith, under the guiding principle of the Three-Self (self-administration, self-support and self-propagation), we try to appropriate positive results of modern Biblical and theological studies in the West, and by integrating with Chinese cultural heritage, seek to develop a theology that is genuinely Christian with Chinese characteristics for the service of the Church in China.

The curriculum consists mainly of disciplines in Biblical, historical and theological studies, as well as practical pastoral training, with supplementary or preparatory courses such as languages (English, Greek and Hebrew) and the humanities. As regards denominational doctrinal and liturgical differences we adopt a principle of mutual respect and an open, positive attitude, ready to learn from and appropriate whatever is helpful to the up-building of the uniting Chinese Church. We also endeavour to strengthen the tie linking the seminary and the church and provide various forms of field work. For spiritual nurture there are private devotional practices, morning and vesper services, and weekly fellowship meetings of sharing. Wide varieties of extra-curricular activities are encouraged to promote balanced growth spiritually, intellectually, physically, morally and socially, and a dynamic spirit of fellowship.

In the past four years 339 students have graduated from the three courses. Some of the graduates stay on to study in the collegiate or graduate courses. Those who left school are now working as preachers or ministers in churches in various provinces, or teaching in other theological schools. In the autumn semester there will-be over eighty new students, chosen from about 350 applicants who have taken the entrance examinations. In 1987 we sent six graduate students of the seminary, three to U.S.A. and three to Canada, for advanced study. In September we are sending five more, one to U.S.A., Canada and Federal Republic of Germany respectively and two to Britain. They will come back to teach in this and other theological schools.

Frequent visits by Christian friends and theologians from other countries provide excellent opportunities for the students to have contact with and understand the situations and trends of development of world Christianity. We are most appreciative of such contacts because they are helpful in cultivating keener Christian experience and promoting friendly relationship.

The Amity Press is a joint effort of the Chinese Amity Foundation and the United Bible Society. The sophistication and modernity of its printing techniques are most impressive, and its general manager, Peter MacInnes, was much concerned that the upheaval in the country not produce a backlash that could restrict the freedom he has had to engage in this vital publishing venture. The regime, in spite of its political repressiveness, offered no resistance to the Bible-publishing operation (how different the days of the Gang of Four!), and believers in China are far better off with 'legal' Bibles from Amity than with contraband Bibles from self-styled Western Bible smugglers and their naive tourist counterparts. Peter is perfectly bilingual, having grown up on the Chinese mission field of missionary parents: an ideal combination of Eastern cultural knowhow and Western technological expertise. Here is his personal description of the Press' work:

Production Update - Amity Printing Press

In the five weeks from April 22 to May 27, the company increased the total number of Bibles printed or in process by almost 87,000 volumes (see chart below). The bulk of these have been the new Simplified Script edition. Also included in this figure are printings for minority Chinese Christians—the Korean Bible for the northeast and the Lisu Bible for Yunnan.

More than 83,000 Bibles have been shipped during this period. The increase in distribution has been greatly facilitated by the Scripture Revolving Fund, providing short-term credit for large shipments, and by the addition of three new distribution centers. The China Christian Council (CCC) now distributes from the Jiangsu Provincial Office, Nanjing Seminary, Hangzhou, and Shanghai. In addition to these centers, the company ships directly to minority centers in Yunnan and Dongbei on behalf of the CCC.

During the second half of 1989 we will print our first pocket-size Simplified Script Bibles as well as Testaments with Psalms. Cooperation with Donghai Press (we will bind and ship what they print) on a low-cost edition of the Old Script Bible will add 100,000 volumes during June and July.

Our most ambitious plans for the second half of the year are to convert the two color presses over to hymnal production. This is in response to repeated requests from the CCC sparked by a growing demand for hymnals. Orders for the rest of the year total 450,000 hymnals, including 150,000 of the badly-needed Little Flock hymnal.

Amity Foundation has begun fund-raising to help underwrite the cost of hymnal paper. The current goal is USD $100,000 annually to cover half the paper costs for one million hymnals.

I send warm greetings and deepest from all involved in this important work. The people in the churches that we hear from are all very grateful for the Bibles they have received.

Best wishes.

Peter MacInnes
General Manager

Total Bibles Since Startup

	04/22	04/29	05/06	05/13	05/20	05/27
Total to Date						
Shipped	636,857	655,807	669,807	679,307	697,881	720,281
Stock	46,318	58,413	55,153	49,977	32,063	57,130
WIP	100,085	69,040	58,300	108,976	108,316	92,756
Total	783,260	783,260	783,260	838,260	838,260	870,167

Nanjing provided an unparalleled opportunity to observe the effect of the Beijing massacre on the average citizen who was not directly involved. First, of course, there was disbelief, reinforced by the totally controlled news presented on government radio and television. The day before the Saturday outrage, the official *China Daily* had reiterated on page one the Beijing municipal government's ban on foreign news coverage of activities prohibited under martial, law (i.e., the student demonstrations in Tiananmen Square).[8] The Saturday issue itself featured an article titled, 'Agencies Say Travel Service Here Is "Normal"'[9]—hardly an accurate description as we ourselves had already discovered!

By Monday 5 June, the government had admitted that something unfortunate had indeed occurred, but the official version would now consistently maintain that (1) only a very few people had been in Tiananmen Square, (2) they had been 'hooligans', not responsible student protestors, (3) *they* (not the army) initiated the violence, and (4) the soldiers who massacred the students were in fact the 'good guys', acting only when provoked, and were the true object of the atrocities! The joint statement of the Chinese Communist Party's Central Committee and the State Council was reported on page one of the *China Daily* on Tuesday, 6 June.[10]

By Thursday, 8 June, the *China Daily* was giving no factual information on the protests at all. Instead, a page one article shifted the focus to the political aspect: 'China Urges US Not To Harm Relations', setting forth the full text of remarks by the spokesman of the Chinese Foreign Ministry who asserted that 'what is happening in China is entirely China's internal affair' and that the Chinese government is 'fully capable of putting down the current rebellion in Beijing'.[11]

Television reporting—which we ourselves watched directly with the linguistic aid of our translator-guides was a perfect illustration of George Orwell's 'double-speak'.

CHINA DAILY

Vol. 9 No.2450 • Tuesday, June 6, 1989 • 2 Jintai Xilu, Beijing • Tel: 583479 Telex: 22022 CNDY CN • Price: 30 fen; 35 fen (airmail)

Statement calls for 'quelling the riot'

The Chinese Communist Party Central Committee and the State Council issued a joint statement yesterday, saying that the Chinese capital is now in a "critical state," as a result of the "shocking counter-revolutionary riot," instigated by a handful of people with ulterior motives, according to People's Daily.

The riot, which began early on Saturday, was aimed at "negating the leadership of the Communist Party, denouncing the socialist system and overthrowing the People's Republic," the statement said.

It was under such circumstances that the People's Liberation Army was compelled to take action to quell the riot. In the course of the action the PLA martial law units "tried their best to avoid bloodshed, but some casualties, nevertheless, occurred, mostly involving military personnel," according to the statement.

The statement urged all Communist Party members, Chinese people from all walks of life and other compatriots to support the Party and government in opposing the riot and help maintain law and order in the city, "but not let themselves be misled by rumours," according to People's Daily.

Also published in yesterday's People's Daily was an open letter addressed to the PLA martial law units by the PLA General Staff, General Political Department, and General Logistics Department, warmly congratulating the units' victory in "quelling the counter-revolutionary riot" and restoring the "honour and order of Tiananmen Square."

However, the letter said this was but an "initial triumph" and urged the PLA units to further consolidate their position and carry on the action against the counter-revolutionary riot to the end, the People's Daily reported.

Soldiers were photographed helping little old ladies across the street; students were made to look like Frankenstein's monster. To be sure, this steady diet of biased coverage could not help but have its impact, especially in a society with a centuries' old practice of accepting governmental authority without question.

But modern communications—thank God—are not monolithic. Short-wave radio could not be controlled, and people listened to the short-wave reports from outside the country and from unbiased sources within it. And students who had escaped the Square left Beijing and told what they had actually seen and experienced; we ourselves talked with some of them. Handbills were surreptitiously printed and distributed everywhere, describing the atrocities. People would line up, blocking the sidewalks and streets, to read the latest privately posted bulletins giving 'unofficial' news. Eventually, the true horror of Tiananmen Square emerged for all to comprehend: some three thousand non-violent demonstrators killed with utter brutality. Now came the symbolic funeral processions, stark in their whiteness, the Chinese colour of death.

At the end of our time in Nanjing we again worshipped with Chinese Christians: this time at St. Paul's Church, a neo-gothic former Anglican church on the Taiping Road. We joined in the singing of 'O Jesus I Have Promised' and 'Bringing in the Sheaves'; the sermon subject was Conversion, and 107 souls were added to the congregation that day alone.

From Nanjing we flew to our final destination in mainland China, the resort area of Guilin, far enough to the south of Beijing to be outside the zone of violence. There we travelled up the fabulous Li River, seeing incredible geologic formations, and visited the magical Reed Flute Cave with its splendid and grotesque stalactites, stalagmites, stone curtains and flowers. But even in this place of extraordinary natural beauty the atmosphere was heavy with the weight of what had occurred in Beijing.

The question now arose as to how we were to leave China. Tourist activity had effectively ceased, and plane schedules were virtually non-existent. There was no possibility of flying to Canton or of going from there to Hong Kong by train as originally planned. The best—perhaps the only—opportunity appeared to be to fly directly from Guilin to Hong Kong, but the national airline of the People's Republic (CAAC) was in no position to carry us. (My wife subsequently purchased a tee-shirt with the inscription: 'I am a CAAC survivor!') The bureau chief of the government travel agency finally told me that the small Hong Kong airline, Dragonair, was more reliable than his own—and he would recommend we work with them!

Fine: all was scheduled for us to depart. But then Dragonair cancelled its incoming flight to Guilin. The airport was bedlam, some passengers convinced that they would never get out of China and that perhaps the government would now turn on foreigners, especially those from countries that had publicly condemned the massacre. But after an additional day's delay, the sleek Dragonair jet swept down; it was well-named, for it looked a bit like a dragonfly. After less than an hour in the air, newly savouring freedom and the glories of French wine as compared with two weeks of doubtful Chinese competitors, we landed in Hong Kong.

CHAPTER TWO

HOW THE WORLD REACTED

Hong Kong

From the medieval squalor of much of rural China to the highrise skyline of Hong Kong is a distance measured not so much in kilometres as in light-years. By concluding our journey in Hong Kong we were able to see the reactions of China's closest western neighbour to the events of 3–4 June.

The shockwaves of Tiananmen Square hit the British Crown Colony with full force. In the days preceding our flight from Guilin, as many as one million people took to the streets in Hong Kong to protest the massacre. Incredibly, this number represented a full twenty per cent of the entire city's population. Businessmen, civil servants, teachers, students, and representatives of the professions took out newspaper advertisements to show solidarity with the protesters in Beijing.

Generally, Hong Kong has had a reputation for nononsense commercialism, not for political activism. Its inhabitants have been too busy making money to become politically involved. Why, then, the staggering reaction to events in Beijing?

Hong Kong is to revert to Chinese control in 1997. Prior to June 1989, that eventuality had resulted in significant emigration from Hong Kong to Canada, the United States and Europe, and in the shift of appreciable private capital out of the Crown Colony. However, nothing resembling a run-on-the-bank had occurred, and though there was dissatisfaction with the details of the transition measures leading from British to Chinese sovereignty and a feeling that the Crown was not pressing as aggressively for the Colony's interests as she should, the overall attitude was one of live-and-let live. Indeed, there were those in Hong Kong who were coming to identify more and more with the mainland—who were beginning to regard 1997 as representing a possibility of—at least culturally—'coming home again'.

But the crackdown in Tiananmen Square changed that perspective forever. When we reached Hong Kong, the persistent sentiment was one of stark terror: 'China today, Hong Kong tomorrow'. If the regime had seen fit to crush protest with such brutality in its own capital, would it hesitate one moment to do so in a city which had already identified itself with decadent western capitalism?

Almost immediately, the topic of migration assumed central importance. At the Australian embassy, for example, the massacre instantly produced a 10–12 per cent increase in the number of emigration inquiries. Two officials on the committee for drafting Hong Kong's constitution after the change of sovereignty (the so-called Basic Law) resigned in disgust. Commented one prominent Hong Kong barrister: 'What's the point of having a Basic Law when you have an administration in Beijing—or Hong Kong post-1997—that seeks to impose its will on the people by military force? It's the emperor's new clothes. Everyone knew it was illusory, but no one dared to say so until now'.[12]

The rosy picture painted by the Beijing government had been that Hong Kong, after 1997, would remain the commercial showcase of the Far East; it would simply function within the larger structure of a benevolent socialist orthodoxy.

I recall five years ago dining in one of my barrister's inns, Middle Temple, London, with a Hong Kong barrister, then humbly doing a pupillage to qualify for the English bar. He was middle-aged, sophisticated, with a beautiful Eurasian wife. Why was he going to uproot and leave the Hong Kong he loved and where he had been very successful? That man had seen the handwriting on the wall: he knew that Hong Kong would soon become a very different place. Events in Tiananmen Square showed that the change was in fact on the doorstep, not a mere remote future possibility.

To be sure, by no means everyone is pulling up roots. We had contact with a Lutheran missionary to Hong Kong, the Reverend Gary Schroeder, who is staying put. Pastor Schroeder is the ideal missionary who thoroughly identifies with the culture in which he is called to operate, and gives his life to those he is called to serve. Perfectly fluent in the exceedingly difficult Cantonese dialect of Hong Kong, he is committed to church planting, evangelism, and Christian education whatever the political vicissitudes. Of course, such a man is drawn to Hong Kong not by materialistic or professional motives but by a transcendental perspective that views political change *sub specie aeternitatis*.

What the Beijing Protesters Wanted

Hong Kong's unqualified condemnation of the 3-4 June repression in Beijing was intensified by the mildness of the protesters demands. It is well recognised in international and domestic law that a government has the right, to keep the peace: to suppress anarchy, affray, rebellion, and unlawful conduct. But those who had been slaughtered in Tiananmen Square—in spite of the herculean efforts of the government to tar them with the brush of 'hooliganism'—had been engaged in conduct of a totally different stripe. What in fact had they been trying to accomplish?

The most important thing to understand in order to comprehend the June uprising was the naive idealism of those involved. In our first chapter, we noted the parallel between Paris in May 1968, and Beijing in June 1989. Though the politics were diametrically opposite, the sentiment was almost identical. At root lay an overwhelming, poignant cry for justice and equity, and an appeal to men of good will to bring it to pass. The Tiananmen Square protesters did not need or want weapons. They believed that the power of goodness would prevail. Gandhi's non-violent protest movement was cut from the same cloth, the vital difference being that his opponents were Englishmen steeped in the high ethics of the western Christian tradition, while the Beijing students faced a totalitarian Marxist government standing in the shoes of millennia of autocratic imperial rule.

Of course, the protesters did have specific demands. At the top of the list was their desire to root out government corruption. As one taxi driver put it: 'We live in hell while the Party leaders live in paradise.'[13] Everywhere we went, everyone to whom we spoke brought up abuse of power by top party officials, and the rampant nepotism exemplified by Li Peng, who as an orphan was raised by Zhou Enlai. Marxism supposedly stood for equality and the rooting out of privilege, but graft and nepotistic aggrandisement reappeared in the Party's own privileged status.

Many of the student protesters had grown up with the elementary school example of Lei Feng—a kind of Chinese Marxist boy scout who lived only to serve the machinery of the Party and do kindly deeds to widows and orphans, etc. 'Learn from Lei Feng teams', they had been told. The hand salute of the Communist 'Young Pioneers' symbolised putting the Party and others before oneself. However, the reality was far different, and the protesters were sick of the contrast between these ideals and self-centred bureaucratic reality.

The protesters also wanted a limited expansion of free enterprise—at least to the point where they could use their abilities in some entrepreneurial ventures. The above-quoted taxi driver bitterly noted that the selfish party leadership could start *their* own businesses: why not other people too? We met students who clandestinely bought goods in Hong Kong or Macao and then resold them in mainland China at a profit. Why shouldn't enterprise be rewarded? The protesters, note well, were not calling for the destruction of the socialist economy; they were asking only for enough economic breathing space to exercise their abilities.

Finally, the Beijing dissidents wanted the society to be opened up to unfettered communication. For a Marxist land, the TV and news publications were relatively enlightened prior to the June crackdown—certainly they were far less repressive and controlled than in East Germany before the Wall came down. But the student protesters had had a strong dose of uncontrolled media reporting through Hong Kong and the ubiquitous shortwave, and they wanted the curtains to be thrown open and the fresh breezes of free speech to waft throughout the land.

In sum, the protesters were very definitely not seeking to overthrow the state or even to eliminate the socialist state philosophy. True, when provoked, they made some untactful, perhaps even rude remarks to and about the Party leadership, but one is impressed by the overall restraint they exercised. For example, listen to a portion of the dialogue of 18 May when Prime Minister Li Peng deigned to visit the hunger strikers;

Li Peng: The Party and the government are really concerned with the student problem. Why, the oldest of you is only 22 or 23! My three children are older. We look at you as our own sons and daughters . . .

Student Leader, interrupting:
> Time is of the essence. We could of course sit around here with a cup of tea, but students are starving. Sorry to interrupt you, but we would like a serious discussion. Let me reiterate our demands. First, we want the student movement to become the object of a positive declaration and the *People's Daily* editorial of 22 April, calling the students anti-socialist and unpatriotic, retracted . . . As a concrete measure, we want Comrade Zhao Ziyang or Li Peng—preferably the former—to answer the students in the Square.[14]

It is noteworthy that nowhere in such exchanges do we encounter the wild rhetoric of the militant revolutionary. The students were looking for openness and understanding. They genuinely wanted to do something for their country, not tear it apart. Only when, finally, the tanks and troops came pouring into central Beijing did they begin to resist with force, and even then their resistance was measured by ordinary standards of self-defence.

It was the common realisation of the protesters' innocence and non-violence that drove the public in Hong Kong to infuriation when they saw the overwhelming eyewitness evidence of brutal governmental repression. Indeed, public reaction was virtually identical around the globe as the full horror of Tiananmen Square became public knowledge.

World Opinion

The vulnerability of the Tiananmen protesters coupled with the overkill of their persecutors elicited a universal outcry from the civilised world.

In the Far East, where political sensitivity is not exactly the defining mark of society, as many as five thousand

Chinese students in Tokyo held a memorial service to condemn the 'criminal acts of the Chinese military'. Three hundred Chinese-Filipinos marched on the Chinese embassy in Manila crying, 'Long live freedom and democracy!' Maoists in Paris did not fare well at a demonstration of some ten thousand protesting the events of 3–4 June: their banner was torn down and they were branded 'Assassins' and 'Fascists'. In London, five thousand Chinese students both from the People's Republic and from Hong Kong marched to the Chinese embassy in a mock funeral procession carrying coffins; their banners read:

DENG = HITLER
and
BEIJING IS A KILLING FIELD

What of official government positions in the wake of the massacre? Here two equal and opposite arguments immediately surfaced. First, there was the viewpoint based strictly on human rights: Beijing should be shown in no uncertain terms that the world will not tolerate such barbaric affronts to human dignity. At the opposite end of the spectrum was the view, ostensively based on long-term diplomatic considerations, that the rest of the world must not isolate China, thereby exacerbating its leaders' tendencies to withdraw into a shell and perhaps engage in even worse repressions.

The 'strong' position was taken in particular by France—quite appropriately in the bicentennial year of that country's Revolution and celebration of the Declaration of the Rights of Man. Foreign Minister Roland Dumas declared that the Chinese government had 'joined a long list of countries that attempt to drown freedom in blood'. France went far beyond other members of the European Economic Community in suspending all official commercial and political contacts with China—not excluding contracts already entered into.

Li Peng's visit to France was summarily cancelled. The French hit, and hit hard: projects such as the $200 million hydroelectric centre in Guangzhou and the building of a nuclear reactor in Guangdong province were stopped dead in their tracks. A month later, on July 14 in Paris, we were privileged to witness Jean-Paul Goude's magnificent Bicentennial Parade, as part of which drum-rolling battalions accompanied Chinese students pushing bicycles and proclaiming, 'We Shall Continue!'

By contrast, Japan's official reaction was maximally diplomatic. While asserting that Beijing had acted 'intolerably from a humanitarian viewpoint', Tokyo suspended only cultural and economic-development missions. Had Japan taken a hard line, China would have been badly hurt, for Tokyo is China's largest trading partner and its largest foreign benefactor ($660 million in aid for 1989 alone).

The United States followed an intermediate course. On the one hand, all military sales to China were frozen (some $500 million in undelivered equipment). At the same time, Washington refused to go further (no embargo on high technology goods or suspension of trade and investment).[15]

What should the proper response have been? In 1985, I chaired a lecture by Prof. Dr. Karl Josef Partsch, distinguished, long-time member of the United Nations' Committee on the Elimination of Racial Discrimination; in passing he dealt with the question of economic sanctions for South Africa.[16] Professor Partsch argued that one of the significant factors that had allowed Hitler to rise so rapidly to power was the virtual isolation into which other nations had placed him. The lesson is surely that we must be careful not unwittingly to create a situation in which totalitarians can function cut off from the rest of civilisation. At the same time, if governments do not object forcefully to human rights violations, their silence will be taken as approval.

Perhaps the American constitutional-law principle of *state action* can help here. In most instances, the U.S. Constitution cannot be employed to limit *individual* unconstitutional actions, for this would impinge on rights and liberties and easily move in the direction of a totalitarian state. But the Constitution very definitely can and should be used to prevent the *state* from curtailing the liberties of its citizens—and the state action rule is violated when the machinery of government (such as the courts) is even indirectly used to further unconstitutional ends (*Shelley* v. *Kraemer*).[17] By analogy, might we not argue that all direct or indirect *government* support for a repressive regime be withdrawn until that government corrects the abuse, but that it is going too far for the state also to attempt to cut off individual and private-sector economic or other contacts with the government in question? In any case, a most difficult balance has to be struck in these cases. Because of the fragility of freedom in the modern world, it *is* clear that where doubt exists, we should certainly come down on the side of freedom and human rights, not on the side of tightrope diplomacy.

The tensions within the U.S. scene on how far to go in establishing sanctions against China have especially surfaced in the question of how to handle students of the People's Republic currently studying in America. Many of these students publicly identified with their counterparts in Tiananmen Square or otherwise made dear their opposition to the repressive actions of their home government. Once their short-term visas run out and they must return to their homeland, what will happen to them? To forestall persecution, President Bush, immediately following the events of June 1989, promised to extend the visas of any of the some forty thousand Chinese students then in the U.S. Japan set forth a similar policy.

But the U.S. Congress, critical of the President's middle-of-the-road initial reaction to the massacre, took the view that the extension of visas by executive action was a woefully inadequate measure. Senator William Armstrong (R-Colo.) spearheaded a bill which would by congressional act have granted any student in America with convincing, documented reason to believe that he would return home to persecution, the right of sanctuary to stay in America. William F. Buckley commented: 'It is difficult to take exception to that very humanitarian impulse of Congress.'[18] President Bush did, however, take exception; on 30 November 1989, he vetoed the legislation, stating that a congressional act would only make his dealings with the Chinese leadership more difficult, and that in any case he was providing immigration guidelines so no student would suffer. Congress was not persuaded, and attempted to pass the bill over the presidential veto. After intense lobbying by the White House, the President succeeded. Congress could not marshall the two-thirds vote required to override the veto. Who was right? The federal law would have been fit and proper, for immigration questions are precisely within the scope of Congressional action, and Deng would have had to live with it! But, pragmatically. President Bush seems to be keeping his word that no Chinese student who is afraid to go home will have to do so. On 11 April 1990, he finally issued the previously promised executive order directing the Attorney General to defer until 1 January 1994 any deportation proceedings against Chinese nationals who were in the United States on or after 5 June 1989, whose visas expire.

Certainly, the safety of Chinese students presently in the United States is of great concern to Americans on all levels. State legislators did not wait for a federal solution to put their position on record. Here, for example, is California's answer:

R. BRIAN KIDNEY
Chief Clerk

October 27, 1989

John Warwick Montgomery
Dean

Dear Dean Montgomery:

I have been directed to invite your attention to Assembly Concurrent Resolution No. 83, relative to the massacre at Tiananmen Square.

Accordingly, a copy of this resolution is enclosed for your information.

Very truly yours,

R. BRIAN KIDNEY
Chief Clerk

RBK:mk
Enclosure

RESOLUTION CHAPTER _____

Assembly Concurrent Resolution No. 83—Relative to the massacre at Tiananmen Square.

LEGISLATIVE COUNSEL'S DIGEST

ACR 83, Hayden. Massacre at Tiananmen Square.

This measure would request that all California public colleges and universities provide appropriate assistance to citizens of the People's Republic of China who have been studying in this state and who fear returning to the danger and repression in their country related to the massacre at Tiananmen Square in Beijing.

WHEREAS, The massacre of unarmed students and civilians by the armed forces in Beijing on June 4, 1989, has been followed by acts of repression throughout the People's Republic of China; and

WHEREAS, Having witnessed the mass slaughter of their fellow students, many of the nearly 3,000 citizens of the People's Republic of China studying at California colleges and universities are afraid to return to their homeland; and

WHEREAS, While the United States government will permit Chinese nationals to remain beyond the expiration of their visas until June 5, 1990, a substantial number of Chinese students who had planned to return prior to the Tiananmen Square horror now face considerable obstacles in their efforts to continue studying in California, including a depletion of financial resources; and

WHEREAS, Students who are forced to return to China may face persecution, arrest, and even execution, in part for participation in peaceful demonstrations in support of democracy and the students at Tiananmen Square; now, therefore, be it

Resolved by the Assembly of the State of California, the Senate thereof concurring, That the Legislature requests all California public colleges and universities to provide appropriate assistance, including visa, residency and asylum counseling, housing and employment placement, financial advising, and psychological counseling, to citizens of the People's Republic of China who have been studying in this state and who fear returning to the danger and repression in their country; and be it further

Resolved, That the Legislature encourages colleges and universities to provide tuition waivers and other financial support to Chinese students who demonstrate emergency need; and be it further

Resolved, That the Chief Clerk of the Assembly transmit copies of this resolution to all institutions of higher education in California.

The importance of California's action does not lie in any legal significance it may have, for matters of immigration are determined strictly on the federal level by virtue of inherent federal power over foreign relations and the plenary power of Congress over aliens. Nonetheless, the California legislature here provides us with a litmus test as to the sentiments of the average American toward possible future victims of the repressive Chinese leadership.

The Aftermath

It is instructive to chart the history of the Chinese political situation in the months that followed the Tiananmen Square atrocity, and the world's reception of the explanations and rationalisations offered by the Chinese government. This can perhaps best be done by a chronological selection of news reports setting forth, where possible, official positions taken by the regime. These reports will be accompanied by brief commentary where their significance is not entirely self-evident.

DEATH SENTENCES GIVEN 3 RIOTERS ON CHINESE TV

BEIJING—Simultaneous campaigns of intimidation and re-education swung into full gear Thursday as millions of Chinese witnessed the televised death sentencing of three participants in a riot and saw soldiers who gunned down unarmed citizens lauded as heroes.

At the same time, the Communist regime stiffened its resistance to economic pressure from the United States and other Western powers, which are attempting to induce China to back away from its repressive tactics.

The death sentences imposed on three men accused of setting fire to a train during a riot in the central city of Shanghai were the first in the widespread recriminations to follow the bloody end of China's democracy uprising.

Lengthy excerpts from the trial, conducted entirely by uniformed police officers in a Shanghai courtroom, were shown on the government's national TV news programme at 7 p.m.

The three men, their hands manacled, entered a dock, one after another, flanked by policemen, and heard an officer charge that they 'frenziedly smashed the railway carriages and set fire to police motorcycles and the carriages. They also prevented firefighters from extinguishing the fire and beat them cruelly.'

The incident occurred June 6, two days after heavily armed troops overran students occupying Beijing's Tiananmen Square and unleashed an orgy of killing that left as many as 3,000 dead in the capital and culminated in its military occupation.

The bloodshed in Beijing set off a wave of violence in cities across China. One of these was the riot near a Shanghai railway station in which a train rammed through a barricade erected by protesters, killing six people.

In violent reaction, the crowd torched the train and beat railway operators, then turned on firefighters.

The three were identified as Xu Guoming, a contract worker at a Shanghai brewery; Yan Xuerong, a worker at the Shanghai No. 18 Radio Factory; and Bian Hanwu, unemployed. They were described as 'criminals' and 'scoundrels'.

In a bizarre touch of Chinese justice, the three were deprived of their political rights in advance of their executions. They were given three days to appeal, but observers said this procedure is just a formality and the executions would most likely be carried out quickly.

The official Xinhua news agency reported that the Shanghai court soon would try seven other defendants accused of similar crimes. More than 1,000 people have been arrested throughout the country.

The ordered executions were the highlight of Thursday's primetime TV newscast. But another example of the orchestrated campaign of intimidation took place on the noon news show, when 26 workers were shown being led by police into a packed auditorium in Changchun, northeast of Beijing.

A number of the workers wore placards hung around their necks, identifying them and stating that they were being sentenced to 'labour reform' for inciting unrest and rumour-mongering.

The use of placards and labour reform were chilling reminders to millions of Chinese of the horrors of the Cultural Revolution, during which teen-age Red Guards terrorised their victims by marching them through streets wearing humiliating signs and dunce caps. Millions were dispatched to the countryside to endure years of virtual slave labour.

Another reminder of that decade, which ended in 1976 when Chairman Mao Tse-tung died and China's current strongman, Deng Xiaoping, succeeded him, is the intensive re-education process now under way.

Thursday's evening news, when it wasn't showing the trial in Shanghai, dwelt almost exclusively on the solicitousness and good deeds of the military. Thousands of soldiers were shown lined up at rigid attention in Tiananmen Square, facing the Great Hall of the People, and being lauded by city officials.

As the martial-law authorities tightened the screws on domestic affairs, other officials claimed that China would resist pressure from the United States and other countries to force it to ease its campaign of repression.

'After the counter-revolutionary rebellion in the Chinese capital was quelled,' Foreign Economic Relations and Trade Minister Zheng Tuobin said at a meeting, 'some governments and a few foreign politicians tried to exert pressure on China and rudely interfere in its internal affairs by such means as halting loans and aid to China and suspending technology transfers.'

This was a direct reference to President Bush's decision to halt the sale of all military equipment in the wake of the violence.[19]

Comment: Here we see the traditional notion of the Marxist 'political trial' in action. The idea is not to get at truth, much less justice for the accused. The purpose of the proceeding is *educative and propagandistic*, not jurisprudential. The accused is an object lesson to the public and a warning as to what can happen if one opposes the party-line. Note that state controlled television is employed to disseminate the lesson (opposition to the leadership = death) to the maximum number of the populace.

CHINA MIND CONTROL HAS ORWELLIAN EFFECT

BEIJING—'What they want to do is make the party line take the place of what's in our minds, to take the place of the truth. They call it "unity of thinking". It must seem strange to you but believe me, it's working.'

The 26-year-old man was explaining a series of meetings, 'study sessions', required for all employees at his government agency.

Such sessions are being scheduled at workplaces throughout China. With an onslaught of TV broadcasts and newspaper articles, they make up an extraordinary campaign by China's communist rulers to control the minds of more than one billion people.

In discussing his study sessions with a US journalist, the young man was taking a grave risk and, therefore, cannot be identified. He described scenes of chillingly Orwellian intimidation, with workers sitting mute and expressionless as superiors lecture them about what thinking is correct and what must be discarded. He said no one looks at anyone else for fear of revealing a telling emotion. No one dares ask a question.

'They say no one was killed in Tiananmen Square. We're supposed to believe that,' the young man said. 'Also, that the military had to come into Beijing to put down a counterrevolutionary rebellion. And that so many people tried to stop them from entering because they were misled by a handful of troublemakers.'

Few believe what they're told at these sessions, which began last week, he said. But there are enough who do particularly older workers who never have questioned the collective wisdom of the Communist Party. No one has yet gathered the nerve to express scepticism.

After attending the hour-long sessions, both morning and afternoon, some workers were beginning to doubt their own beliefs.

'I myself am not influenced yet, but a lot of people are confused,' the young man said.

'You must bear in mind that the true believers are still in power. My division chief is one of them, and he conducts the study sessions. Those who don't believe don't have any power. They're the ordinary people, like me. As long as they control my job, my housing, my food, my chances for advancement and benefits, my entire life, there's not much I can do to resist.'

One purpose of the mind-control campaign is to get people to inform on one another.

'In my apartment building,' he said, 'the old cleaning women are suddenly asking questions about whose son may have been present when an army truck was burned somewhere or whose brother may have marched in a protest demonstration on such and such a date.'

Many of his colleagues were swept up in the effervescence of the protest demonstrations and the sit-in at Tiananmen Square. They painted banners with pro-democracy slogans and marched in a large, chanting group.

Many were photographed and videotaped by plainclothes police officers. They knew it, but such was their enthusiasm that they thought of themselves as invulnerable.

Now they know better. And they're frightened.

'Everyone is afraid of being checked closely for what we did during the demonstrations,' the young man said.

The techniques of the study sessions vary.

'Some units have had to list the names of people who participated in the demonstrations,' he said. 'Most people are keeping silent, not telling what they know. But some have already criticised themselves. Some say they now realise that what they did was wrong, and they hope that by confessing they'll get off easier than if they wait to be accused.'

One of his colleagues who organised a protest march is expecting arrest. Many more anticipate a loss of privileges or a transfer to a remote part of the country.

The thought-control campaign is reminiscent of the Cultural Revolution, a tumultuous decade that began in 1966 when Chairman Mao Tse-tung unleashed the frenzy of teen-age Red Guards. Then, the mind-conditioning catechism was the little red-covered book of Mao's quotations.

Today's gospel is a speech delivered by Deng Xiaoping, on June 9, when he congratulated senior army commanders for crushing the democracy movement.

Parts of the speech were broadcast on state-run television that night. A full text never has been published. Instead, successively shorter versions have been relayed down the Communist Party hierarchy, and brief excerpts are used as the basis for the study sessions.

Out of Deng's speech has emerged the core of the party line:

'This disturbance is independent of man's will. The very small number of people first staged turmoil, which developed into a counterrevolutionary rebellion. They are attempting to overthrow the Communist Party, topple the socialist system and subvert the People's Republic of China to establish a bourgeois republic.'

Why the entire speech has not been released, apparently not even at the highest echelons, has baffled observers. But a Communist Party member who heard an abbreviated, 20-minute version said the original apparently made references to how close Deng's hard-line leadership came to being toppled and how indebted he was to the army.[20]

Comment: Orthodox Marxism has had a long history of rewriting history and programming the people to believe the current official version of past events. Thus, after the fall of Beria, the *Great Soviet Encyclopedia* substituted an article on the Bering Strait, effectively relegating Beria to non-existence![21] Here, the Party leadership operates on the solipsistic theory that truth is entirely plastic and that people can be made to believe anything if it is reiterated enough and the social consequences of not believing it are made sufficiently frightening.

PEKING BLAMES 'AGENTS' OF TAIPEI

China yesterday accused Taiwan 'special agents' of stirring up unrest and working for the downfall of the Communist Party in Peking as seven more people were executed for their parts in the prodemocracy protests.

Seventeen others were executed in China, but their sentences were not thought to be related to the protests.

Chinese evening television news gave details of eight people, all mainland Chinese, who had been arrested as Taiwan agents. According to the report, two had been caught in Peking, two in Shanghai, two in Guangdong, one in Ningxia, and one, who had given himself up, in Liaoning.

The detained men, who are mostly in their twenties and thirties, include workers, factory officials and one journalist.

The journalist is based in Shanghai and although the newsreader did not announce which paper he worked for, a picture of the *World Economic Herald* offices was flashed on the screen. This paper has been criticised for its attacks on government policy.

All the 'agents' were said to have been recruited either inside China or on trips abroad.[22]

Comment: It is standard procedure to find a foreign scapegoat for a mess such as occurred 3–4 June 1989. Taiwan was a particularly good choice, since its alignment with the U.S. made possible simultaneous criticism of American policy toward China.

POLICE WIDEN THEIR HUNT

Police raided six Beijing university campuses On Friday, arresting at least 17 teachers and students and searching for an equal number of others in the nationwide hunt for fugitive activists in the movement, Chinese sources told United Press International.

Chinese sources on Beijing campuses said policemen seized four persons from the Beijing Film Institute, ten at the Beijing Normal College of Physical Culture and one from the Political Science and Law College. Two were arrested at the Beijing Institute of Foreign Languages, the sources said.

The *People's Daily* would not say what had happened to its former director, Qian Liren, or to its former editor. Tan Wenrui. Both apparently lost their jobs because of the relatively independent path that the newspaper tried to pursue for a time in May, and perhaps because reporters of the newspaper were openly demonstrating for freedom of the press.[23]

PRESIDENT OF BEIJING UNIVERSITY REPLACED

BEIJING—The government Wednesday replaced the president of Beijing University, China's most prestigious academic institution and the vanguard of the democracy movement during the spring.

Former President Ding Shisun was regarded as a protector of his students, and his dismissal was forecast widely by students and faculty.

The official New China News Agency quoted Ding as saying he' had asked to leave the post as early as February 1988 for 'health and other reasons'.

Ding, 62, a mathematician, was replaced by Wu Shuqing, 56, former vice president of People's University in Beijing. People's University has strong connections to the Communist Party.

The change comes at a time when the educational programme at Beijing University is undergoing a major overhaul to instill more communist values in students and teachers.

At Wu's inaugural ceremony, He Dongchang, vice minister of the State Education Commission, said he hoped Beijing University would 'adhere to a socialist orientation' and train a large number of 'expert personnel who have both ability and political integrity', the news agency reported.[24]

Comment: Educators and journalists are particular threats to a totalitarian regime. Here, above all, thought-control must be complete.

CHINA READIES NEW ATTACK ON DISSIDENTS

BEIJING—Chinese authorities are preparing to launch a new wave of arrests of alleged 'counter-revolutionaries' who supported this spring's student-led democracy movement, an official newspaper reported Sunday.

As part of a continuing effort to track down and arrest the most active members of the protest movement, all Beijing residents will be required, starting Friday, to carry their personal identification cards whenever they leave their homes, the government-controlled *Beijing Daily* reported. Checks of motor vehicles and drivers' licences also will be stepped up, the newspaper said.

'Counter-revolutionary elements have hot been thoroughly cleaned up, and motor vehicles often are used as tools of crimes', the newspaper said. 'Therefore, the martial-law troops and police must, according to the law, strengthen inspections of motor vehicles and drivers.'

Reports of Attacks on Troops

Persistent reports have circulated among Chinese citizens and diplomats in Beijing that scattered incidents of violent attacks on martial-law troops, including drive-by shootings of soldiers, have taken place this summer.

Dozens of semi-automatic weapons are believed to have fallen into the hands of protesters during the chaotic night of June 3–4, when soldiers shot their way into Beijing, killing hundreds, perhaps thousands, of people who sought to block their path. Diplomats and Chinese have expressed belief that some of these weapons have been used in late-night attacks on soldiers.

The number of martial-law soldiers standing 24-hour guard at bridges, intersections and in the embassy district has been reduced in recent weeks, and at least in the daytime, a superficial calm has settled, over the city. But the sound of gunfire still is sometimes heard late at night. It is seldom possible to learn who fired the shots or why.

Martial-law troops still stand guard at Tiananmen Square, the central site of the pro-democracy movement. Vehicles, including bicycles, are allowed to pass the square, but pedestrian traffic is barred except for those with special permission to sightsee.

Many Remain Angered

Government propaganda has sought to portray the brutal June 3–4 suppression of the protests as a necessary and proper response to a 'counterrevolutionary rebellion'. But many people remain deeply angered by the killings.

In recent days, there have been various signs that hard-liners in the government—presumably aware of the failure to convert most city residents to the official view of events—have been preparing to take more severe measures.

Some intellectuals and government critics have shown indications of growing fear for their own personal safety or career positions.

A Western businessman in Beijing said that Chinese friends recently told him that military bases north of the city have been prepared to receive an expected wave of new detainees, some of whom might be subjected to political indoctrination and 'labour reform'. Friday evening, there were exceptionally large-scale movements of canvas-covered military cargo trucks in the city, most of them apparently empty but some carrying soldiers.[25]

CHINA OUSTS ITS CULTURE MINISTER, APPOINTS HARD-LINER

BEIJING—Minister of Culture Wang Meng, who for three years presided over a gradual liberalisation in Chinese arts, has been fired, and a leading hardline official has been appointed to act in his place, Chinese media announced Monday.

The official New China News Agency reported that Wang, 54, a respected author, had asked to step down 'to concentrate on writing and literary criticism.'

But Wang's removal, which had been rumoured for days, is widely viewed as part of a continuing purge of reformist officials associated with former Communist Party General Secretary Zhao Ziyang, who was removed from his post in June after opposing the use of martial-law troops to suppress student-led pro-democracy demonstrations.

In a related development, news services reported that the governor of Hainan province, Liang Xiang, has also been fired. Liang, 70, also an associate of Zhao, is the highest-level provincial official to be removed from office.

Western diplomats said his firing would have implications for foreign investors and for China's economic reforms, because Hainan had been chosen to take the lead in the country's experiments with capitalistic forms of trade and investment.

The pro-Communist Hong Kong newspaper *Wen Wei Po*, which reported Liang's dismissal

Sunday, said the governor is under investigation for corruption.

Wang's replacement apparently will be He Jingzhi, a recently appointed vice minister of culture, who is a poet but whose reputation is primarily that of a hard-line propagandist.

He Jingzhi, who most recently has been deputy head of the Communist Party Propaganda Department, had served previously as a vice minister of culture. He was reappointed to that post last week and was also named acting head of the ministry, state-run television reported Monday.

He also has been named head of the Communist Party structure within the ministry.

Wang, who became minister of culture in 1986, encouraged a loosening of controls on literature and the arts. Among the most dramatic symbols of the new openness were several controversial art shows in Beijing during the last year, including one devoted entirely to paintings of nudes.

He Jingzhi, in contrast, has been a leading advocate of ideological orthodoxy. He played key roles in promoting a 1983 campaign against 'spiritual pollution' and an 'antibourgeois liberalisation' drive in 1987. Both campaigns were aimed at attacking Western influences.

New Wave of Criticism

Since this June's crackdown against pro-democracy demonstrators, and Zhao's fall from power, a new wave of criticism has been launched against pornography and any literature viewed as advocating allegedly decadent foreign life styles. This new campaign now is likely to get a further boost from He Jingzhi.

'Literary and art circles are part of the ideological front,' He Jingzhi declared in an April 1987, speech, during the height of that year's antibourgeois liberalisation campaign. 'Our opposition to bourgeois liberalisation is aimed at strengthening our Marxist world outlook and our Marxist concept of literature and art . . . We must advocate depicting the bright side of things and depicting advanced and heroic figures. Only by doing so can we inspire the people to stride forward.'

He Jingzhi is considered a protegé of former Propaganda Minister Deng Liqun, a hard-line ideologue who has been in semi-retirement since 1987 but who remains one of the orthodox figures most feared by reformist intellectuals.

Some Chinese say that Deng, who was removed from the Communist Party Central Committee in 1987, has recovered considerable political clout since the June crackdown.[26]

CHINESE VOW TO PURGE COMMUNIST PARTY

BEIJING—Leaders in the Beijing Communist Party voted Sunday to purge the party of 'hostile and antiparty elements' and wealthy private businessmen, whom they called exploiters.

The decision, reported by the official Xinhua News Agency, indicated that the harsh crackdown triggered by student protests in June is not winding down after nearly five months, but rather will be intensified.

Also Sunday, an official report said lawmakers have proposed banning Hong Kong residents from anti-government activities after the colony reverts to Chinese rule in 1997.

Xinhua said the Beijing party committee, which has led the nation in hard-line rhetoric, approved a resolution to 'purify the party organisations' by requiring all members in the city to re-register next year.

Only those who meet party qualifications will be retained, it said.

'A drive will be conducted to examine and investigate how party members, especially officials with a party membership, behaved in ending the national turmoil and quelling the anti-government rioting,' it said, referring to pro-democracy protests that the army crushed in June.

'The overwhelming majority of the party members will be united and educated and a very small number of hostile and anti-party elements will be resolutely purged from the party,' it said.

It did not say how many of Beijing's ten million residents are party members or how many are expected to survive the examination. So far, only a few expulsions from the party have been announced, including that of Yan Jiaqi, a political scientist who fled to the West in June and is working to organise opposition from overseas.

Former party General Secretary Zhao Ziyang, ousted for allegedly supporting the student protests, has been allowed to keep his party membership, but some top officials are believed to be pressing for his expulsion. He already has lost all party posts.

Leading targets of the party purge include private businessmen.

'The resolution stipulated that exploiters cannot be admitted into the party, and those who have already been party members must adhere to the party's ideals,' it said.

'Besides getting their own due pay, they should spend their post-tax profits on production and public welfare and should not use them for their own private needs. If they fail to do so, they can no longer be party members,' it said.

Private businessmen were commonly described as 'exploiters' during the first three decades of Communist rule, but after senior leader Deng Xiaoping began reforming the centralised economy a decade ago, they were embraced as partners in China's modernisation.

At least one millionaire was admitted to the party.

Since the June crackdown on the student movement, however, hard-line policies have made a comeback in all areas.

Party leaders have begun criticising private businessmen for becoming wealthy.[27]

CHINA SAYS FOREIGN INVESTMENT HIGHER

BEIJING—*China Sunday* announced a rise in foreign investment this year despite a nation-wide crackdown on student-led protest, but diplomats said fear of economic and political instability was scaring investors away.

The *China Daily* quoted figures from the Ministry of Foreign Economic Relations and Trade (MOFERT) as saying foreign investment in the first nine months was $2 billion, up 29 per cent on the same period last year.

'Although some politicians in the West have encouraged economic pressure on China, the business community has paid little heed,' it commented. 'The attitude seems to be that business opportunities must be seized or lost forever.'

Western governments, Japan and the World Bank suspended new loans to Beijing after troops and tanks crushed student-led protest on June 4, killing hundreds, perhaps thousands of people. Nationwide arrests of those involved continue.

A Western diplomat said foreign firms had 'been shocked by the events, making them nervous about China's political stability, although the effect might not appear until the investment figures in 1990.

'Firms are not reassured by the rhetoric that the open-door policy will continue. They are looking for concrete steps that the reforms are going on. But decision-making is becoming more secretive. Beijing is reverting to planning methods, not the market, to solve its problems,' he said.

He said economic policy was taking second place to ideology. 'Why come to China? There is intense competition for investment dollars from other countries in the region.'

A second diplomat said foreign firms believed Chinese workers were less motivated than before, with more time allocated to political study.[28]

CHINA SANCTIONS UNRAVELLED

WASHINGTON—President Bush's sanctions against China for the massacre in Tiananmen Square began falling by the wayside months before last weekend's surprise visit to Beijing by White House national security advisor Brent Scowcroft.

Bush imposed the restrictions June 5 'to express the outrage we feel' over the bloody crackdown, but they began to dissipate as early as August, a check of the purportedly affected programmes has shown.

A spokesman for The Boeing Co. said three Boeing 757–200 commercial jetliners initially held up by the president's announcement were delivered to China in August, a delay of only a month in the original schedule.

Boeing also was allowed to send a fourth 757 in August, apparently without any delay, and an even bigger 747 passenger jumbo jet to Beijing in October.

Shipments of the jets were supposed to have been suspended because their navigational systems have potential military uses.

So were three communications satellites being built by the Hughes Aircraft Co., and due to be launched in China. Work on all three satellites is continuing under special approvals and 'preliminary licences' apparently granted in September to allow exchanges of data with the Chinese.

Bush continued to encounter stiff criticism for opening the door for renewed relations with China. Rep. Sam Gejdenson (D-Conn.), chairman of House Foreign Policy subcommittee on international economic policy and trade, Tuesday said, 'In China, where the government has only tightened the screws, the Bush administration seems to see no limit on what they ought to try to do to help the Chinese government.'[29]

BEIJING RESIDENTS SAY CRACKDOWN CONTINUES

BEIJING—While Washington state business representatives and their Chinese hosts were busy making plans for the biggest-ever Sino-U.S. trade conference in the United States, a middle-aged professor a few blocks away was being questioned about his activities during last spring's pro-democracy demonstrations.

'Every faculty member has to go through it. We call it an introspection session,' the professor said today as he expressed relief that his answers were accepted the day before by the thought police. 'The repression now is even tougher than under martial law.'

Armed troops are no longer standing guard on street corners throughout this sprawling capital city, but many Chinese and Western residents agree that a harsh climate of repression remains. And many of those believe it is getting worse.

That poses a dilemma for state business representatives who have agreed to sponsor up to 500 Chinese next October at a controversial trade conference in Seattle. It will be the largest such gathering in the history of Sino-U.S. relations. But critics view it as an effort by Beijing to buy respectability in the aftermath of June's Tiananmen Square massacre.

Despite assurances from their Chinese hosts that harmony and stability have returned to China, some members of the 16-person delegation remain unconvinced.

'I feel like we're going around here in a glass bubble,' one participant said in the hectic round of meetings, factory tours and banquets. 'We don't really know what those people out there in the streets are thinking.'

The professor, who requested anonymity, said mass resentment is boiling just beneath the surface, forcing the Communist regime to keep the lid on tight while trying to project an image of normalcy.[30]

A TENSE TIME FOR CHINA

BEIJING—Word of the execution of Romania's communist strongman Nicolae Ceausescu last

Christmas Eve raced through the *People's Daily*, the mouthpiece of the Chinese Communist Party, and created a startling scene in the company cafeteria.

Suddenly, spontaneously, scores of workers began banging their metal dishes with their spoons, creating a deafening uproar.

It was, said a person who witnessed it, 'awe inspiring'.

There is no question that news of this symbolic insurrection at an institution inseparably bound to the Communist Party reached China's aging leadership within minutes, confirming its worst fears.

'The military kept the party in power in Romania,' a Western diplomat said last week. 'And then the military turned on the party...

'Ceausescu was one of their (the Chinese leaders') last friends in the world. Then they saw pictures, in living colour, of him lying in a pool of his own blood.'

These are fretful times for the tight little group of senior leaders who make all the important decisions about how to run this country of 1.1 billion people.

One by one, the communist regimes of Eastern Europe have toppled like little red dominoes. Now even the Soviet Union, birthplace of the political system that in its various forms has controlled the lives of 35 or 40 per cent of humanity for the last 40 years, has forsworn the doctrine of Leninist infallibility, and with it the Communist Party's monopoly on power.

Now another spring is on its way to Beijing, bringing with it the memories of last year's unrest.

To make certain there is no repetition of those events—which began with the death of the ousted reform-minded Communist Party chief Hu Yaobang on April 15 and ended when the tanks roared down Changan Avenue to Tiananmen Square on June 4—the government has intensified its efforts to prevent the formation of any network of students or workers big enough to organise a demonstration.

'If any large group of people gets together they're simply hauled off,' a Western diplomat said.

Last week, the Chinese Communist Party released a document addressing the leadership's newest concern, the same army that suppressed last year's demonstrations. The paper called for tighter political control over the military, including the promotion of officers based on political reliability rather than skill.

All 48 million members of the Communist Party—whose ranks were filled with supporters of the students last spring—are being evaluated.

They have been required to write about where they were during the demonstrations, what they thought and their attitudes toward party doctrine. It is a test all but the dimmest—or those known to have participated in the demonstrations—pass with ease. But it is intimidating.

Though the Chinese government released 573 people arrested as a result of last year's unrest, estimates of those still detained run as high as 30,000. At least twenty have been executed.

As a result, on the vast expanse of Tiananmen Square, where last year it seemed that anyone who could speak English could hardly wait to air his grievances, not a soul approaches.[31]

CHINA'S COMMUNIST PARTY MOUTHS SLOGANS OF SUPPORT FOR 'THE MASSES'

BEIJING—China's Communist Party, increasingly isolated as communism loses its grip as far away as Eastern Europe and as close as Mongolia, laid out a plan for its political survival at the end of a key meeting yesterday.

The party revived a 1960s Maoist call to unite with the masses, saying it had become separated from the people because of 'bureaucracy, subjectivism, formalism, passivism, corruption and other serious phenomena'.

'Adhere to the practice of "coming from the masses and going to the masses,"' a statement carried by the Xinhua news agency said. Party leaders were told to 'go down to the grassroots units and go among the masses.'

Diplomats described the statement, issued at the end of a four-day Central Committee plenum, as a return to language inspired by Chairman Mao Zedong during the 1960s when people did not dare challenge the authority of the party.

They questioned whether such slogans would help the party under 85-year-old senior leader Deng Xiaoping heal the wounds inflicted by the army's assault on pro-democracy protesters in Beijing's Tiananmen Square last June.

Party leader Jiang Zemin and Premier Li Peng made what the agency called 'important speeches' but did not reveal the contents. No mention was made of last year's protests and no personnel changes were reported.

The statement's only reference to the dramatic events sweeping the East Bloc—and now, on China's doorstep, Mongolia—was a reference to 'a changeable world situation'.

The statement said that despite the changes and 'temporary domestic difficulties', the 1990s would be a decade of victory for China as it marched along the road of 'socialism with Chinese characteristics'.[32]

SANCTIONS AGAINST CHINA, NEVER STRONG, ARE ERODING

BEIJING—Citing national interest, humanitarian causes and business competition. Western democracies are slowly dismantling the sanctions they imposed on China after the bloody suppression of the democracy movement last June.

Western officials are coming back to renew contacts with Chinese counterparts, but tourists and business people, still apparently wary, haven't returned in the numbers in which they came before.

The West remains committed, in principle, to limits on high-level visits, arms sales and new aid packages. But with the beginning of the year 'exceptions' have become the rule and some sanctions, never strong to start with, are withering away even though repression continues.

The turning point was the surprise visit in December by U.S. National Security Adviser Brent Scowcroft and disclosures that he had made a previous visit in July, just a month after the army killed hundreds, perhaps thousands, of people in smashing the pro-democracy movement.

President Bush was assailed in Congress for his overtures to the hard-line Beijing government, but other Western nations quickly followed suit in easing bans on high-level contacts.

But the tourists and business people who had poured into China after it opened up to the West a decade ago are staying home.

Tourist-hotel occupancy rates are only about half what they were a year ago, and the China market seems to have lost its lustre for businesses as the government reasserts central controls and puts off new market-oriented reforms.

'Businessmen were the first to argue we really ought to get back in,' said an Australian diplomat. 'Now they are some of the most reluctant to come back.'

John Frisbie of the U.S.-China Business Council said: 'There is little direct correlation between sanctions and business, but the direction of Chinese policy was positive before. Now businessmen are uncertain and will be for some time.'

The renewed contacts are chiefly governmental. The most important outcome of those contacts, to China, has been the lifting of bans on credit and aid.

In December, the European Economic Community gave its twelve member nations the go-ahead to extend export credits to China, and Spain responded by announcing a $30 million development loan in early January.

On February 2, the U.S. Export-Import bank signed a $9.75 million loan with a Chinese oil corporation. A week later the bank announced a $10.4 million grant, part of a $23.1 million package to encourage China to buy American equipment for a Shanghai subway project.

The bank said contracts won by American companies would have been jeopardised if financing had not been completed. West Germany has provided $275 million in preferential credit for the subway project.

Only a few private syndicated loans have been made since June but, as one West German diplomat said, 'Everyone is waiting for the World Bank.'

The Chinese 'are almost passionate about World Bank loans,' said one U.S. official. He said Chinese officials constantly bring up the $780 million in World Bank concessionary credit suspended since June and blame the United States for it.

'They say, "If the World Bank loans do not come through, we will retaliate against you,"' the official said.

On February 8, the World Bank, after a White House decision to back loans for 'human needs', approved a loan package of $30 million to aid an earthquake-struck area of northern China.

The bank, with 151 nations as members, is still withholding the big development-loan package, but a positive decision could open the floodgates, particularly from China's main creditor, Japan.

Japan continues to discourage commercial lending but has also given the go-ahead to 'human need' loans and has started talks on a five-year, $5.6 billion package of development aid.

Other signs of encroaching normality in relations are showing up. A $600 million U.S. project to develop avionic equipment for Chinese fighter planes is on course, and Chinese engineers were allowed to return to their jobs at U.S. plants in October.

A vote by the U.S. Congress in late January to codify sanctions drew howls of protest from China, but Congress allowed Bush to waive sanctions if doing so were in the 'national interest'. The president exercised that right in approving the export of three U.S.-made satellites to be launched by Chinese rockets.

The U.S. Department of Agriculture recently authorized China to buy an additional one million metric tons of wheat at subsidised prices. U.S.-China trade in general expanded by nearly 40 per cent in 1989 over 1988.

Bush and other Western leaders have argued that the Chinese people should not suffer from sanctions and that it's bad policy to isolate the Chinese government. So far, however, China has done little to reciprocate the West's conciliatory gestures.

The government, in moves mainly intended to improve its image and obtain badly needed foreign credit, lifted martial law in Beijing in January and announced the release of 573 participants in the pro-democracy movement.

But political repression continues, with dissent outlawed and thousands of activists languishing in jails without being formally tried.[33]

DENG STEPS DOWN FROM LAST POST

BEIJING—The resignation of senior leader Deng Xiaopeng from his last governmental post, as chairman of the state Central Military Commission, was accepted today by China's national legislature.

The expected move followed the 85-year-old Deng's retirement last November from the Communist Party's Central Military Commission, a body with largely the same functions as the state commission. That was his last party position.

Deng, who came to power in the late 1970s and initiated market-oriented economic reforms that helped modernise parts of China, is still regarded as the nation's most powerful man.

Deng was not present at the National People's Congress session today, and did not attend the opening of the annual meeting yesterday. The Congress acted on a letter from the party Central Committee saying that Deng had resigned from the party military commission.

The letter noted that party General Secretary Jiang Zemin had been appointed to succeed Deng as chairman of that commission.

Jiang, Deng's chosen successor after the fall of party chief Zhao Ziyang last June, is also expected to be appointed head of the state military commission, a powerful body responsible for defence policies.

Although Deng now holds no party or government posts, he is believed still to have the final say on major decisions and plays a key role in maintaining the outward impression of harmony among Beijing's various leadership factions.

Deng has sought to set an example for other aging leaders by stepping down from public office and encouraging the promotion of younger leaders. He resigned from the Politburo Standing Committee, the party's top decision-making body, in 1987.

However, he and other more conservative octogenarians have not relinquished their behind-the-scenes authority, and have played an instrumental role in the revival of ideological orthodoxy following the suppression of the prodemocracy movement last spring.[34]

Comment: With some exceptions, pressure from the West to alter the Chinese situation after Tiananmen Square has been largely ineffective. The existing gerontocracy, with the army behind it, has tightened ideological control at all points.

The remarkable changes in the U.S.S.R. and the collapse of totalitarian, doctrinaire Marxism in Eastern Europe have not phased the Chinese ruling clique. Deng's retirement does not signal any meaningful changes: he made very sure that his policies would continue in the person of his successors. With the execution of Nicolae Ceausescu, China has now become the last significant bastion of hardline Marxist orthodoxy.

How is this possible, when the collapse of the Gang of Four and the opening of China through Nixon's visit seemed to herald China—certainly not Russia—as the enlightened socialist regime of the future? To understand this mystery, we must better comprehend the world-view of Marxism and see its relationship to the traditional Chinese value-system.

CHAPTER THREE

MARXISM IN CHINA

*T*o understand the tragedy of Tiananmen Square, one must understand the nature of Chinese Marxism. And to understand Chinese Marxism, one must go back to the roots of classical Marxist theory, for, with the current radical changes occurring in the U.S.S.R. and Eastern Europe, China represents the last important refuge of traditional Marxism in the world today. Once we have taken a critical look at Marxist orthodoxy and its official role in the People's Republic, we shall compare it with the new approach of *glasnost* and *perestroika* characteristic of Gorbachev's Russia, and ask the key question; why has such a programme been rejected in China?

Classical Marxism

Political philosopher George Catlin has neatly summarised the essential elements of the orthodox Marxist world-view:

> Together Marx and Engels, by a combination of Jewish rabbinic subtlety and German industry, built up a philosophy which in its involved consistency has no compeer since St. Thomas laid down his pen. For it the Communist Manifesto provided the Prophecy and *Das Kapital* provided the Torah, the Law. Here is 'the Book'... This Marxian philosophy is a coherent whole. It is massive because revolutionary action is built upon class-war theory; the class war upon the

> economic theory of surplus value; this economic theory upon the economic interpretation of history; this interpretation upon the Marxo-Hegelian logic or dialectic; and this upon a materialistic metaphysic.[35]

Marxian *materialism* is not static—not mechanistic as was the materialism of the ancients, of Hobbes, and of Condillac. Marx condemned such materialism as not taking into account free will and dynamic energy, and adopted Hegel's *dialectic interpretation of history* 'with considerable changes, to be sure, in its supposed metaphysical implications but with no important change in the conception of it as a logical method'.[36] What, then, is the dialectic interpretation of history? Essentially this: every tendency when carried to the full (thesis) breeds an opposite tendency (antithesis), which combines with the thesis to form a new tendency (synthesis). The synthesis then becomes a new thesis, and the dynamic process begins anew. The conflict of two opposites never results in the complete annihilation of either; out of the conflict always emerges the synthesis which, while leaving elements of both thesis and antithesis behind, yet embodies the truth contained in each.

Obviously, two different interpretations of these dialectic processes are possible; the emphasis may be on continuity—the impossibility of making radical and voluntary departures from the past; or it may be upon discontinuity—the necessity of continual break with the past. Whereas Hegel emphasized continuity in this historical 'spiral that mounts as it turns', Marx emphasised discontinuity and revolution—'the continual swing of social theory between revolutionism and revisionism'.[37] A further difference between the Hegelian and Marxian dialectic lay in metaphysical assumption: Hegel's essentially idealistic belief that history was the progressive realisation and materialisation of the World Spirit in time, was vehemently rejected by Marx. Marx and Engels were dialectic *materialists*, not 'bourgeois' idealists;

'In Hegel's hands,' claims Marx, 'dialectic underwent a mystification.' The laws which Hegel 'first developed in all embracing but mystical form,' Engels explains, 'we made it our aim to strip off this mystic form and to bring clearly before the mind in their complete simplicity and universality.' Putting the matter somewhat more picturesquely, Marx asserts that 'In Hegel's writings dialectic stands on its head.' It 'is upside down,' Engel elucidates, 'because it is supposed to be the "self-development of thought," of which the dialectic of facts is therefore only a reflection, whereas really the dialectic in our heads is only the reflection of the actual development which is fulfilled in the world of nature and of human history . . .' 'You must turn it right way up again,' admonishes Marx, 'if you want to discover the rational kernel within the mystical shell.'[38]

Despite their materialism, Marx and Engels, like Hegel, saw a truly moral necessity in the development of civilisation through the dialectic process. To Hegel, the expansion of the inner forces of civilisation meant a powerful and united German state; to Marx it meant the inevitable success of the proletarian revolution. Marxism has always seen the dialectic process as more than a working hypothesis; were it not a method of historical interpretation which makes prediction possible, the proletarian revolution would lose its essential inevitability.

Marx' *economic interpretation of history*, the third essential element in his system, may be stated very simply: the economic factor is the key to the dialectic process. To Marx and Engels, an analysis of economic trends and movements rewards the student with an understanding of the course which history will take; for the thesis, antithesis, and synthesis which create the upward spiral of civilisation are economic in nature. Some writers have claimed, it is true, that

Marx did not make the course of history completely dependent upon economics, but such interpretation is refuted both by the logic of Marxism (Marx derived his messianic view of the proletarian revolution solely from an economic interpretation of the dialectic process), and by a consideration of innumerable statements from the writings of both Marx and Engels:

> Our conception of history depends on our ability to expound the real process of production, starting out from the simple material production of life, and to comprehend the form of intercourse connected with this and created by this (i.e., civil society in its various stages), as the basis of all history; further, to show it in its action as State; and so, from this starting-point, to explain the whole mass of different theoretical products and forms of consciousness, religion, philosophy, ethics, etc., etc., and trace their origins and growth, by which means, of course, the whole thing can be shown in its totality (and therefore, too, the reciprocal action of these various ideas on one another) ... It does not explain practice from the idea but explains the formation of ideas from material practice; and accordingly it comes to the conclusion that ... not criticism but revolution is the driving force of history, also of religion, of philosophy and all other types of theory. It shows that ... at each stage there is found a material result: a sum of productive forces, a historically created relation of individuals to nature and to one another, which is handed down to each generation from its predecessor; a mass of productive forces, different forms of capital, and conditions, which, indeed, is modified by the new generation on the one hand, but also on the other prescribes for it its special character.[39]

> The materialistic concept of history starts from the proposition that the production of the means to support human life and, next to production, the exchange of things produced, is the basis of all social structure; that in every society that has appeared in history, the manner in which wealth is distributed and society divided into classes or orders, is dependent upon what is produced, how it is produced, and how the products are exchanged. From this point of view the final causes of all social changes and political revolutions are to be sought, not in men's brains, *not in man's better insight into eternal truth and justice, but in changes in the modes of production and exchange.* They are to be sought, not in the philosophy, but in the economics of each particular epoch.[40]

The complex and highly technical *theory of surplus value* shows *how* the distribution of wealth determines the course of history. The capitalist, according to Marx, continually drives the wages of his employees down to subsistence level in order to cut his labour costs and obtain the cheapest labour. Capital, by its inherent desire for economic domination, becomes more and more concentrated: organised trusts replace small businesses, and more and more efficient machines come to be employed. Thus the worker is continually paid less for running his machine, while at the same time his machine becomes more and more productive through improvement and replacement. Since, according to Marx, in a perfect competitive system the real value of a product is the value of the labour put into it, a vast discrepancy arises between the wages which the worker receives and the real labour value of the commodities which he produces. This difference—which is appropriated or stolen by the capitalist—is what Marx termed 'surplus value'. Yet the capitalist is little better off than his employees: since the capital—'constant capital'—produced by his machines is only sufficient for their own repair and replacement, the capitalist experiences a falling rather than a rising profit rate as his machines increase in number and his workers decrease in number. Only surplus value is profit for the capitalist, and surplus value cannot be extorted without workers; yet the capitalist must decrease rather than increase wages in order to have money for fixed capital, without which he will fall behind in the production race. The lumbering capitalistic monster advances to its own destruction—a destruction preceded by many workers unemployed and the rest working for practically nothing; few capitalists owning tremendous factories filled with machines which yield practically no profit.

The intolerable situation described here obviously means a violent change in the existing structure of society. The dialectic process grinds to a stop with the *class-war* between proletariat and capitalist—a struggle which results in the final overthrow of capitalism both economically and politically. The State itself with its legal machinery—the instrument of capitalism—'withers away', and the proletariat ceases to exist once the means of production falls into the hands of the, workers.[41] After a literal 'dictatorship of the proletariat' of indefinite length,[42] during which time the final vestiges of capitalism are destroyed, the golden era of the *classless society* is ushered in'.[43] Marx asserted that the active and revolutionary opposition of the proletariat would be required in bringing the capitalistic era to a close; thus the evangelistic emphasis in the concluding section of the *Communist Manifesto*:

> In short, the Communists everywhere support every revolutionary movement against the existing social and political order of things . . . The Communists disdain to conceal their views and aims. They openly declare that their ends can be

attained only by the forcible overthrow of all existing social conditions. Let the ruling classes, tremble at a Communist revolution. The proletarians have nothing to lose but their chains. They have a world to win. Working men of all countries, unite![44]

Marxism Weighed in the Balance and Found Wanting

Before examining Marxist orthodoxy in China, let us critically evaluate the remarkable world-view just described. The inherent problems with classical Marxist theory must be understood in order to appreciate the collapse of Socialist governments throughout the Eastern bloc and the new face that Marxism now displays in Gorbachev's Russia. The cardinal Marxist principles treated above will be critically examined in the order presented: the materialistic metaphysic; the Hegelian dialectic; the economic interpretation of history and the surplus-value theory; class-war and the dictatorship of the proletariat; and the ultimate classless society.

Materialism. Materialism is the linchpin of the entire Marxist world-view. Elsewhere I have endeavoured to provide a philosophical/theological refutation of this foundation stone of all classical Marxism. Since 'in a materialist theory there are no necessary beings and no supernatural interventions in the course of nature' and since 'materialists must show there is no reason to believe in survival of bodily death',[45] my approach has been to offer primary-source, historical, non-hearsay, eyewitness evidence—at the level of the legal test of 'moral certainty, beyond reasonable doubt'—in support of the miraculous intervention of God in Jesus Christ into human history and his proof of life after death through his resurrection from the dead.[46] If Christ did in fact miraculously conquer death, materialism cannot possibly be true.

Moreover, from a purely methodological standpoint, as McDougal, Lasswell, and Chen observe;

> It has become increasingly clumsy to divide all factors in psychological and social processes into the 'material' and the 'nonmaterial'. A two-term system can, of course, be made to serve some purposes of investigation. However, its utility is modest in any case, and the hazards of rigidifying an entire approach into empty verbal dialectic are greatly increased in such a limited system.[47]

And 'rigidity' and 'emptiness' are by no means the worst of the deleterious consequences of the materialistic interpretation of human affairs. The Marxist has an overwhelming tendency to relate all human conduct to material considerations, thus trivialising human activity and the actors in the human drama. We are told that 'great composers like Bach could not even have expressed their genius if they had had nothing to eat'. Such arguments miss the point that though eating is a necessary condition to explain human conduct, it is by no means a sufficient explanatory factor.

Materialism so skews the overall picture of human life that it cannot avoid diminishing the importance of the ideological and spiritual dimensions of man's existence. Nothing could be more serious where human rights are concerned, for the neglect of civil liberties and the transcendent will assuredly dehumanise the citizens of any nation. It is still an empirical truth that 'man does not live by bread alone'.

The Dialectic Process. Marx, in turning Hegel's idealistic dialectic on its head, nevertheless retained one of Hegel's most fundamental conceptual errors: the assumption that a dialectic process (whether idealistic or materialistic in nature) must move onward and upward to a positive goal. In reality, the dialectic is no more than a formal principle of interacting opposites which neither discloses the goal of the process nor places any value judgement upon it. The dialectic can describe a continual refinement of evil as well as a continual refinement of good. Nothing about the dialectic itself necessitates the attainment of a classless society (or, for that matter, Hegel's idealistic goal of freedom).

Why did Hegel and Marx gratuitously assume that progress was built into the dialectic and thus into human history? For the simple and understandable reason that they uncritically absorbed the progressivistic, optimistic, evolutionary mindset of the nineteenth century—which in turn had secularised the biblical promise of a divine goal to history and was living off its inherited capital.[48] But today's Marxist, enmeshed in the twentieth-century world of global wars, genocidal death camps, and potential nuclear holocaust, no longer has any sociological justification for holding to Marx' unverifiable dialectic hope. Absent any transcendent, divine word to the contrary, the interaction of secular opposites can as readily lead to a hell on earth as to Utopian bliss. If one is oblivious of this fact, one can grossly neglect the preservation and promotion of those human rights which spell the difference between Milton's *Paradise Regained* and Orwell's *1984*.

Economic Reductionism. No intelligent person doubts the importance of economic factors in life, and Marxism deserves much praise for redirecting the attention of modern man to the pervasive effect of economics on all aspects of societal activity. Nonetheless, 'the adequate performance of the scientific task is thwarted by exaggerated deference to the weight of the economic variable. Explanations that stress the predominating significance of a single causal factor are in a peculiarly vulnerable position as knowledge advances'.[49]

In point of fact, the economic aspect of life is but one way of looking at the total human condition—one of many spotlights (such as the political, the educational, the cultural, the religious) in the light of which man's experience can be better understood and hopefully ameliorated. Trouble arises the moment any one of these factors is elevated to the status of the necessary explanation or source of all the rest. Such reductionism warps the nature of human experience and often results in superficial solutions to profound problems. To take a homely example: economic difficulties are probably a fruitful source of marital discord; but it does not follow that once a couple's budgetary problems are solved they cannot find other sources of conflict (nor does it follow that only the marriages of the poor and the exploited break up).

Class-War. Karl Löwith makes the related point that 'even if we assume that all history is the history of class struggles, no scientific analysis could ever infer from this that class struggle is *the* essential factor that "determines" all the rest'.[50] Historical events since Marx' day have belied his prophecy that only revolution against capitalism will satisfy the proletariat. Labour unions and governmental anti-trust and anti-monopolistic legislation have given workers such a high standard of living in the West that good television reception is closer to their hearts than a forceful overthrow of society! Here, again, Marx was a victim of the limited historical perspective afforded by his nineteenth-century society.

Class-war, we are told, will inevitably usher in the dictatorship of the proletariat, and then that final form of the state will in turn 'wither away'. The fact that orthodox Marxism places a positive value on dictatorship, however temporary it is supposed to be, leaves one with feelings of deep disquiet as to the seriousness or practical significance of its verbal crusades against tyranny and human rights violations.

The Classless Society. The eschatological hope of Marxism displays Communism's ambiguous, confused view of human nature. For Marx and his followers human beings are evil exploiters of one another (they manipulate unjust economic systems of their own creation to the detriment of their fellows and for personal gain), and yet they are capable of an idyllic, classless existence once a suitable economic environment is provided.

Plainly, a new human nature is required for such a goal to be realised. But, as G. W. Smith of the University of Lancaster argues, 'once the thesis as to the largely social nature of personal identity is annexed to the idea that involuntary social relations are abolished in communism, the possibility of accounting for the enduring individual seems to evaporate'. He continues:

> Liberals often accuse Marx of suppressing the individual in the name of communal solidarity, and they typically see this suppression as taking the form of forcibly subordinating the individual to the general will. Those Marxists who do not profess to disdain individual liberty usually reply by maintaining that, on the contrary, individual liberty is fully and completely realised only in communism. Both parties in fact badly underrate the conceptual revolution implied for our inherited ways of looking at ourselves and others in Marx's metaphysics of freedom. To claim that the individual is neither suppressed nor liberated in communism because he cannot conceivably exist there in the first place is perhaps excessive, but the exaggeration might at least serve to raise a question rarely asked with seriousness,

namely: in what way is the 'new man' of communism recognisable as a man!⁵¹

The only answer appears to be that he is unrecognisable, for he represents a qualitative transformation for which we lack any historical example. Moreover, though he is analogous to a religiously reborn person, no divine grace operates as the effective agent in re-creation and no divine Saviour serves as a model of what this rebirth would practically signify. Once again, Marxism displays itself as a secular religion, trying to have the benefits of a new creation without the presumed disadvantages of a transcendent Redeemer.[52]

For political scientist Eric Voegelin, that Marxist effort at 'immanentising the eschaton' is the unpardonable historical sin. He terms it *metastatic gnosis*: the notion that 'the Christian idea of supernatural perfection through Grace in death [should be] immanentised to become the idea of perfection of mankind in history through individual and collective human action.'[53] And he illustrates how natural it is for men who play God to do it badly—to tyrannise over their fellows and lose all respect for human dignity. Utopianism is a dangerous plaything, especially where human rights are concerned.[54]

A Closer Look at 'The Party'

In Jack Higgins' novel *Solo*, the following exchange takes place between a revolutionary activist and her nemesis, a SAS officer:

> Lieselott Hoffmann turned on Morgan and raised a clenched fist. 'Power to the people.'
> 'Which people, you silly little bitch!'
> She lowered her hand, a strange uncertainty on her face . . .[55]

Lieselott's uncertainty could well have a basis in what Chalidze refers to as Socialist legal dualism:

> ... dualism in the sense that the state is governed both on the basis of procedures regulated by laws and by the Constitution, and on the basis of procedures regulated by Party law and not by state legislation ... The withering away of the state is characterised by a shift from the former 'bourgeois' state to the present Party-state dualism in law, with a subsequent shift to a purely Party direction of society without any state apparatus.[56]

The standard approach of orthodox Communist government in the period of the dictatorship of the proletariat (and this is the only empirical stage practical Marxism has ever reached) is to place the interests of the people in the hands of the Party leadership, which best insures their true welfare. Ironically, a revolutionary movement holding high the banner of 'the people' leaves the populace with fewer protections and less say in the conduct of their lives than did the allegedly repressive system it replaces.

The consequences for society are not difficult to see. Thus under Marxism the implementation of fundamental Socialist rights

> ... is permitted only in the interests of the workers. This thesis results from the task to be performed by fundamental rights, namely to further social development, which in socialism serves the interests of the workers. To refer to fundamental rights in any other context would be unconstitutional. The socialist interests of the working people constitute the inherent limitation on all fundamental rights. The communist party decides what is in the

> interest of the workers, because it is composed of the most progressive and responsible representatives of the working population and is therefore able to comprehend best their interests as well as the objective laws of social development... According to the Eastern concept the substance of fundamental rights changes in the course of the dialectical process of history in conformity with the prevailing economic conditions. In a socialist society they are subject to the constitutional proviso relating to the interests of the working population. These interests are crystallised in the consciousness of a small minority, the communist party. The day-to-day political objectives of the party constitute the inherent limitations of fundamental rights, which on this basis may be restricted at will or even completely abolished.[57]

Philosopher Cornelius Murphy makes the powerful point that the absence of legal and political accountability in such a system constitutes an irremediable affront to human rights and fundamental freedoms:

> In Marxist-Leninist ideology, a regime of the rule of workers is projected as a political ideal. It is as the representative of the working class (industrial and/or rural) that the ruling elites in socialist countries justify their political power. It is demonstrable that such a hypothesis can be a facade for tyranny, but in philosophic terms, the weakness of the theory runs deeper.
>
> The flaw lies in the assumption that political authority is vested in *one part* of the body politic. It is probably true that some of the major transformations of social existence will, in the foreseeable

future, result from the political action of alienated groups. But it is important to distinguish between a *political movement* and political authority. The energies of a limited number may provide the impetus for change, but their leadership does not divest others of their right to participate in political processes and to demand an accountability from whomever may govern . . .

The importance of this question can be better understood where its implications are drawn to mind. The possession of political authority by all the people includes the corollary that all have a right to call government to account. Accountability is assured not only through periodic elections, but also by the voice of criticism. Liberty of expression is essential to a free people, especially as it may be directed towards those in power. Criticism, as well as sovereignty, belongs to all; human rights cannot flourish unless everyone, and not just members of a particular class have a right to speak on public issues.[58]

Today's China and Classical Marxism

During the decade of the so-called 'cultural revolution' (1966–1976), the Marxist leadership of China, represented by the 'Gang of Four', established an incredibly repressive society in China: the legal system was literally abolished, churches were closed, and all dissent was ruthlessly eliminated. Can we conclude that the overthrow of the Gang of Four meant the creation of a less orthodox Chinese Marxism?

The answer is a resounding negative. The post-cultural-revolution leadership has—in typical Marxist fashion—rewritten the history of that decade so that the Gang of Four become 'counter-revolutionaries': traitors to true Marxism! An official publication puts it this way;

> The undermining activities of the two counterrevolutionary cliques, headed by Lin Biao and Jiang Qing respectively, brought the biggest setbacks and losses to the country since the founding of the People's Republic. In October 1976, with the overthrow of the counterrevolutionary clique headed by Jiang Qing, China entered upon a new historical period.[59]

The 'new historical period' from 1976 to the present did indeed represent an opening of the country to foreign industry and trade, to greater communication with the outside world, to the restoration of a formal legal system, and to a less repressive attitude toward religion. However, all this was done in the name of Mao Tse-tung, the symbol of pure Chinese Marxism.

How orthodox was Mao's interpretation of Marxism? The most careful study to date of Mao's thought shows him to have been primarily an activist—the developer of novel strategies in the practice of revolution—rather than an original thinker. He was generally satisfied to reiterate, albeit in homey, peasant-like discourse that appealed to his Chinese audience, the ideas of Marx, Engels, and other classic Soviet writers.

> To say that he is a poor philosopher is not to scoff at his achievement, but to see it in a better light. Mao Tse-tung has attained his highest distinction as a Communist revolutionary leader. He fought a long guerrilla war brilliantly and made an enormous nationalistic peasant revolution work well ... But he has attained no real distinction as a great

theory-maker unless 'theory' is taken to mean political stratagems rather than basic abstract principles. Thus he has not changed such basic concepts as production, accumulation, surplus value, exploitation, and economic determinism; he has merely repeated Lenin's emphasis on political control in discussing these concepts. He has provided no fundamentally new interpretation of any other basic principle in Marxist-Leninist theory but rather a gloss on some, particularly on the matter of rural revolution...

With respect to the dictatorship of the proletariat, Mao has not changed Lenin's view of the important concept, but has added the national bourgeoisie to the group of classes retaining political rights. The national bourgeoisie continues to be a suspect class and capitalists' property and minds are to be converted into state property and the 'collective' mind.[60]

In short, even though there is truth in the view that Mao, and the China so deeply influenced by him, rejected 'bloc thinking' (in contrast with the Russians), and that the Chinese brand of Marxism has a pragmatic, *Realpolitik* character,[61] the fact of the matter is that Mao and his followers have made every effort to maintain a strict, classical, orthodox Marxism.

Evidence of a prevailing Marxist orthodoxy in China in the years that have followed the end of the 'cultural revolution' is especially plain when one examines the role of the Party and its leadership. The government cheerfully characterises itself as 'the People's democratic dictatorship', referring to the fundamental Marxist-Leninist motif of the dictatorship of the proletariat:

> The People's Republic of China is a socialist state under the people's democratic dictatorship led by the

> working class, and based on the alliance of workers and peasants. People in the country enjoy democracy while the state adopts strict measures to protect them from subversive elements. Hence the term 'people's democratic dictatorship'.
>
> Workers, peasants, intellectuals, and all patriots who support socialism and also those who work for the unity of the motherland belong to the category of the people . . .
>
> In China, the working class exercises its leadership through the Communist Party.[62]

Noteworthy here is the paternalistic, protectionist philosophy so characteristic of orthodox Marxism. 'Democracy' in no sense means government *by* the people; it signifies government *for* the people. The people are to be 'protected from subversive elements', i.e., anything that would lead them away from the political orthodoxy imposed upon them. The term 'people' does not mean all citizens; it embraces only the 'patriots who support socialism'. Thus, by definition, Marxism is always the belief-system of the people! And, just in case there should be any room for ambiguity or ideological slippage, the will of the people is expressed through the voice of the Communist Party.

Indeed, as we have already seen (chapter one) by way of the reactions of a typical Party member to the repression of the students in Tiananmen Square, the true 'voice of the people' narrows even more: the *leadership* of the Party imposes its will upon the country even in the face of the majority of Party members. One might diagram the strict orthodoxy of Marxist political theory in today's China by a series of concentric circles, representing the bizarre fact that the 'people' are ultimately narrowed and redefined until only the central Party leadership has the say as to what is the will of more than a billion citizens!

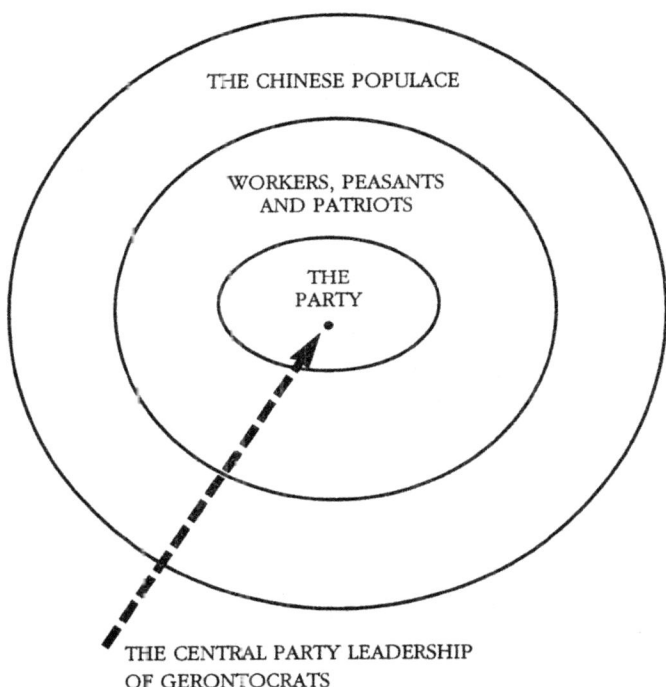

The legitimacy of this interpretation of present-day Marxism in China is particularly evident when one looks at the jurisprudential aspect of Chinese society. Following the demise of the cultural revolution in 1976, a formal legal system was reintroduced into China, law schools were reestablished, and the legal profession again commenced to function. Did this mean the protection of civil liberties and the general manifestation of the 'rule of law' as distinct from arbitrary rule through personal or political power?

This exceedingly important question has recently been addressed in a law-review essay on 'The Promise of Law for the Post-Mao Leadership in China'. The author, a specialist in the fields both of law and of East Asian studies, notes that the post-Mao law reforms had a twofold aim, viz., greater democratisation and greater centralised economic development—thus raising the question as to how two such potentially conflicting aims could be reconciled. Her sad conclusion is that in China 'law will strengthen the leadership of the party'.[63]

This comes about because law reform has now placed the lower-level Party members (the 'cadres') under the law, instead of permitting them to carry out government policy arbitrarily, according to their own lights. True, this means that the petty bureaucrats can be brought before the courts when they misuse their power. The problem is that the central Party leadership is not *also* brought under the rule of law.

> With law, party cadres could be removed from government administration without ever threatening Central Party leadership. By strengthening the legal system. Central Party leadership would be reinforced at the same time that democratic rights of the people were expanded. In the process, the role of non-Central Party members would necessarily diminish . . .
>
> In sum, then, laws would communicate the policy of the Central Party down through the ranks and out to the branches of government. No longer would party cadres be responsible for determining the correct routes or interpreting Central Party policy for their own units. Theoretically there would be no 'indigenous' variations of the policies sent down from the Central Party. Law would provide a unified package of messages from the Central Party to all locations. Propagation of law would strengthen the Central Party's position and thus ensure that China's modernisation would reflect socialist values.[64]

And what occurs if one opposes Party policy as established by the central leadership—or even their style of governing—as did the protesters of 3–4 June 1989? The answer is all too clear in the provisions of the new Chinese criminal code dealing with 'Crimes of Counter-revolution':

> *Article 90* A 'crime of counter-revolution' refers to any act that is committed with the aim of overthrowing the political power of the dictatorship of the proletariat and the socialist system and endangers the People's Republic of China.
>
> *Article 91* Whoever colludes with a foreign state in plotting to jeopardise the sovereignty, territorial integrity and security of China shall be sentenced to life imprisonment or fixed-term imprisonment of not less than ten years.
>
> *Article 92* Whoever plots to subvert the government or dismember the state shall be sentenced to life imprisonment or fixed-term imprisonment of not less than ten years.[65]

In its handling of the Tiananmen Square protest, Deng and company acted in complete consistency with the style and principles of classical Marxism: deviation from Party policy, as established by themselves for the good of the people, must be ruthlessly suppressed.

A New Wind Blows: Mikhail Gorbachev

Just before the 3–4 June massacre, Gorbachev made a state visit to Beijing. His schedule was continually changed by his hosts to keep him away from the protesters, whose banners pictured him as 'Pioneer of Glasnost' and 'Emissary of

Democracy'. Gorbachev's remarks on that occasion were carefully and diplomatically chosen so as not to create a rupture with the Chinese leadership (he has since been severely criticised by many for not unambiguously supporting the students), but it was clear from what he did say that he saw in the protest a viewpoint far more compatible with his own than that represented by his official hosts. How does the new approach of Gorbachev, which is revolutionising his own nation and has already freed Eastern bloc countries from oppressive regimes, differ from the orthodox Marxism of China's leadership? Let us hear in extenso from Gorbachev himself, as he gives us the historical background of *glasnost* and *perestroika*:

> What is perestroika? What prompted the idea of restructuring? What does it mean in the history of socialism? What does it augur for the peoples of the Soviet Union? How might it influence the outside world? All these questions concern the world public and are being actively discussed. Let me begin with the first one...
>
> All honest people saw with bitterness that people were losing interest in social affairs, that labour no longer had its respectable status, that people, especially the young, were after profit at all cost. Our people have always had an intrinsic ability to discern the gap between word and deed. No wonder Russian folk tales are full of mockery aimed against people who like pomp and trappings; and literature, which has always played a great role in our country's spiritual life, is merciless to every manifestation of injustice and abuse of power. In their best works writers, filmmakers, theatre producers and actors tried to boost people's belief in the ideological achievements of socialism and hope for a

spiritual revival of society and, despite bureaucratic bans and even persecution, prepared people morally for perestroika.

By saying all this I want to make the reader understand that the energy for revolutionary change has been accumulating amid our people and in the Party for some time. And the ideas of perestroika have been prompted not just by pragmatic interests and considerations but also by our troubled conscience, by the indomitable commitment to ideals which we inherited from the Revolution and as a result of a theoretical quest which gave us a better knowledge of society and reinforced our determination to go ahead.

The life-giving impetus of our great Revolution was too powerful for the Party and people to reconcile themselves to phenomena that were threatening, to squander its gains. The works of Lenin and his ideals of socialism remained for us an inexhaustible source of dialectical creative thought, theoretical wealth and political sagacity.

His very image is an undying example of lofty moral strength, all-round spiritual culture and selfless devotion to the cause of the people and to socialism. Lenin lives on in the minds and hearts of millions of people...

The policy of restructuring puts everything in its place. We are fully restoring the principle of socialism: 'From each according to his ability, to each according to his work', and we seek to affirm social justice for all, equal rights for all, one law for all, one kind of discipline for all, and high responsibilities for each. Perestroika raises the level of social responsibility and expectation. The only people to resent the changes are those who believe that they already have what they need, so why should they readjust? But if a person has conscience, if he does not forget about the good of his people, he cannot—and must not—reason in such a way. And then glasnost, or openness, reveals that someone enjoys illegal privileges. We can no longer tolerate stagnation . . . The restructuring effort started with the Party and its leadership. We began from the top of the pyramid and went down to its base, as it were. Still, the concept of 'revolution from above' doesn't quite apply to our perestroika, at least it requires some qualifications. Yes, the Party leadership started it. The highest Party and state bodies elaborated and adopted the programme. True, perestroika is not a spontaneous, but a governed process. But that's only one side of the matter.

Perestroika would not have been a truly revolutionary undertaking, it would not have acquired its present scope, nor would it have had any firm chance of success if it had not merged the initiative from 'above' with the grass-roots movement; if it had not expressed the fundamental, long-term interests of all the working people; if the masses had not regarded it as their programme, a response to their own thoughts and a recognition of their own demands; and if the people had not supported it so vehemently and effectively . . .

Having adopted at the 27th Congress the concept of a contradictory but interconnected, interdependent and, essentially, integral world, we began to build our foreign policy on this foundation. Yes, we remain different as far as our social system, ideological and religious views and way of life are concerned. To be sure, distinctions will remain. But should we duel because of them? Would it not be more correct to step over the things that divide us for the sake of the interests of all mankind, for the sake of life on Earth? . . .

Universal security in our time rests on the recognition of the right of every nation to choose its own path of social development, on the renunciation of interference in the domestic affairs of other states, on respect for others in combination, with an objective self-critical view of one's own society. A nation may choose either capitalism or socialism. This is its sovereign right. Nations cannot and should not pattern their life either after the United States or the Soviet Union. Hence, political positions should be devoid of ideological intolerance.[66]

What do we learn from these arresting passages? First, that, unlike the Chinese leadership, Gorbachev is genuinely concerned with the international situation and with global (not mere national) health. Second, that he sees an open society as an asset, not a liability. From the recently established Western-style parliament, presidency, and elective system in the U.S.S.R., with corresponding de-emphasis on the influence of the non-democratic Communist Party, we now know that Gorbachev's *glasnost* entails a movement away from Party dictatorship. Thirdly, Gorbachev plainly hates bureaucracy, inequitable Party privilege, and governmental corruption.

At the same time, the above-quoted passages make equally clear that Gorbachev sees his reforms as stemming directly from and being thoroughly consistent with the beliefs of Marx and Lenin. Indeed, the radical changes he has brought about were motivated primarily by *materialistic, economic considerations*—in perfect accord with the fundamental perspective of Marxism.

Two Chinese analysts write of his work:

> The advancement of Gorbachev's 'new thinking' is closely related to the economic situation in the Soviet Union. Since the mid-1970s, the Soviet economic growth rate has been on the decline. According to official Soviet statistics, during the ninth five-year plan period (1971–75) national incomes were increasing at the comparatively fast rate of 5.1 per cent. But during the tenth five-year plan (1976–80), the rate fell sharply to 3–9 per cent and in the eleventh five-year period (1981–85), it dropped further to 3.2 per cent... He was concerned that if such a situation persisted, the Soviet Union might not be able to maintain its status as a major power. A sense of crisis about the prospects of the Soviet Union forced Gorbachev to make drastic reforms to the Soviet economic system. To achieve this he needed a comparatively relaxed international environment.[67]

The 'mixed' character of Gorbachev's operation (interlacing Marxist and Western values) makes him hard to evaluate both in his own circles and in ours. Among hardline conservative Christians and political rightists, his Marxism requires a hidden 'conspiracy theory' explanation for whatever good he may be doing: he is really trying to get the West to put its military guard down so that he can conquer capitalism through subtlety and guile; indeed, he may be the very Antichrist who will unite all peoples as a secular saviour! At the opposite pole, there are Christian believers who, seeing the incredible increase in freedoms he has brought about in Eastern Europe, regard him as a crypto-Christian (after all, he was baptised as an infant and has a believing mother!). A more balanced approach theologically, we suggest, is that of common grace: just as God used Pharaoh and Nebuchadnezzar to do his will, so he uses even unbelievers today to carry out his purposes to increase freedom and human dignity on the earth.

The Chinese have likewise had difficulty knowing how to react to Gorbachev. The protesters idolised him; the leadership clearly rejected his philosophy of glasnost. Why the rejection, since the Chinese leadership could certainly have justified accepting him on the basis of his clear commitment to Marxist-Leninist materialism and economic determinism?

Several reasons enter into the equation.

(1) The sheer size of China and its population provide the Chinese leadership with an excuse to focus solely on their national interests. Gorbachev's concern with internationalism and preserving the globe from destruction means little to them. To them, the international scene offers economic opportunities for China: little more.

(2) The age of the Chinese leadership. Deng and company are not prone to consider new perspectives. Hardening of the arteries has become also hardening of the categories.

(3) China was in such utter primitivism before the Communist takeover in 1949 that the current leadership can point to incredible progress under orthodox Marxist, repressive leadership. Thus there is little incentive to change. (Understandably, the student protesters had far more contact with the outside world and its values than the average Chinese, and so could see the awesome disparity between a still backward China and the West.) The U.S.S.R. itself had been virtually impervious to Western capitalist and democratic ideas until the spectre of economic collapse united with modern satellite communication with the West drove Gorbachev to 'new thinking'.

(4) The 'imperial mindset'—of which we will have much more to say later—has given millennia of Chinese an authoritarian attitude: blind acceptance of arbitrary dictatorial power. In reality, there was no 'Last Emperor': the current Marxist leadership functions as imperialistically as did the ancient emperors. The Cult of Mao differed in no important respect from the hoary Cult of the Emperor. Such a mindset on the part of ruler and people does not mesh very well with *perestroika* and *glasnost*.

(5) Finally (and this takes us to the following two concluding chapters for this section of the book), the traditional religions of China have offered no incentive toward democracy, civil liberties, or social justice. A strong statement, but, sad to say, a truth nonetheless. Perhaps a different belief system is capable of producing the change of perspective so desperately needed in today's volatile China.

CHAPTER FOUR

CHINA'S RELIGIOUS HERITAGE

One of the most distinguished twentieth-century sinologists is John King Fairbank, professor of history at Harvard University. Professor Fairbank writes:

> Another part of China's heritage from her past, which lies behind modern authoritarianism, was the particularly passive attitude of non-officials toward government, the apparent irresponsibility of the individual citizen toward affairs of state. Sun Yat-sen complained that his people were like 'a heap of loose sand'. Many writers used to deplore the selfish opportunism, competitive jealousy, and disregard for others which they discerned in individual conduct outside the bond of family, clan, and personal relations. It is a perennially fascinating paradox—this contrast, to the Western way of thinking, between loyalty to family and friends and disregard of the public interest, between the most meticulous sense of responsibility, when responsibility was customarily expected and clearly undertaken, and a callous irresponsibility regarding the suffering of strangers or public evils that concerned no one in particular.
>
> Obviously this unwestern ideal of conduct springs partly from the fact that the family has outweighed the

> community both as an object of loyalty and a source of benefits. *But the secret of this paradox undoubtedly lies also in the passive and individualistic aspects of China's religions. This passivity complements, and also conduces to, authoritarian government.*[68]

There is no doubt that an important connection exists between the present-day authoritarian Marxist regime, in China and the religious history of the Chinese people. To understand the nature of this relationship, we must look both at the traditional faith of the people and at the three great religio-philosophical belief systems that have coloured China's historical development (Taoism, Confucianism, and Buddhism).

Traditional Chinese Religion

In the West, if one excludes primitive, pre-civilised cultures (the Europe of the druids. North America before the arrival of the white man), religion may most readily be studied as the history of competing doctrines or institutions: Judaism, Islam, Catholicism, Protestantism. Folk religion is an interesting; but by no means central, concern. Not so in China. 'Religiously the Chinese have been very eclectic. In proportion to the total population, the number of simon-pure Buddhists, Confucianists, or Taoists has been comparatively small . . . In this eclecticism the Chinese were by no means always critical. The masses particularly often held at one and the same time reciprocally contradictory views.'[69] In a number of ways, the folk religion of China says more about the mentality of the people than the far better known classical religions of that land.

Perhaps the term 'religion' is inappropriate for the folk beliefs so characteristic of the long history of China. 'Superstition' might be a more accurate designation. Here, for example, is a descriptive summary of the prevailing religious atmosphere during the Han dynasty (202 B.C.–A.D. 220):

> Many elements can be distinguished in the religious and superstitious beliefs and practices of Han China. There was a deep-seated belief in prognosticating the future; men tried to serve the spirits of their departed ancestors, to placate beings which were thought to be malevolent and to accord due reverence to personified powers of nature. There was a faith in the protecting powers extended by Heaven to the emperor and his dispensation; but at times of political intrigue, attempts were made to interfere with the imperial succession by means of imprecation. A yearning for immortality expressed itself in a number of forms. Some theorists had explained the creation of the universe and the operation of its natural cycles as the result of two overwhelming forces [*Yin-Yang*] and their interaction with the material elements of which the world was composed; and a faith in these doctrines persuaded some of the need to regulate their behaviour and to adopt symbolic patterns so as to comply with these inescapable rhythms. In some areas, particularly in the south, there survived local practices of a dubious nature, which involved a trust in intermediaries and the contacts they made with occult powers through trance or ecstasy . . .
>
> One of the nine major departments of the Han government was concerned with matters of religion, and its complement included special officials who were responsible for prayer, the upkeep of shrines or similar duties. The attention of the state to these matters was no innovation of the Han house, but came as an heritage from the pre-imperial kingdoms; for

these had been no less anxious to secure earthly blessings from unseen powers . . . The government . . . took a hand in prescribing the rites that were to be performed in honour of the spirits, or to appease those powers thought capable of making or marring human happiness. The state provided for shrines to be built to honour the lords of the rain or the winds, or the guardian spirits of certain holy rivers or mountains. Each locality in the empire was commanded to conduct its own worship and sacrifices to the local protecting spirits and to maintain the intermediaries by whose agency man could make contact with the occult. These spirits included the lords of the soil and of the crops, who were entitled to receive seasonal reverence and offerings of sheep or swine.[70]

Especially noteworthy here is the early blend of gross superstition and the occult with religious practice, and the government's overall, umbrella-like influence and control over religious activity.

But, surely, it will be argued, such popular beliefs have little to do with the enlightened China of today. Remarkably, the popular religion of twentieth-century China has more affinities with that of the Han period than with the religions of the West! What are its characteristics?

First, there is de facto polytheism. A gigantic pantheon of deities has been the object of Chinese worship through the centuries. Chamberlain discusses nineteen of the most influential—including such fascinating specimens as Kuan Yin, the 'Hearer of Cries', and Tao Hua Hsien Nii, the 'Peach Blossom Girl'—but these are only a fraction of the gods who can be placated to make life more bearable. This uncritical polytheism displays itself today in the simultaneous worship of mutually inconsistent gods of the major religions:

> A friend told me the following story. When she was young her family rented two rooms from an elderly woman. Every Sunday this woman would disappear to the New Territories. One day she asked the woman where she went. The woman told her of the religious group to whose ceremonies she went. They worshipped five Gods—Lao Tzu, Buddha, Confucius, Allah and Christ![71]

Secondly, Chinese folk religion yesterday and today contains the powerful element of ancestor worship. Let us hear again from Chamberlain:

> Funeral services at the time of the Shang dynasty were lavish and involved the interment of horses, carriages, vessels as well as of wives. The more important the person, the more people were buried along with him. This was done on the grounds that he would need them in the other world. Also he had to be kept happy for his powers to inflict punishments or grant favours greatly increased after death.
>
> If we compare this with the present day, burning of 'hell money', paper houses, cars etc., there is little basic difference. The dead exist and have to be accorded their due ...
>
> Today, ancestor worship takes a variety of forms. In some households there is a scroll with the names of the ancestors on it. This is often placed in the West hall (the hall of Autumn) and the period of worship covers the first half of the seventh month.
>
> There are also the visits to the graveyard at the festival of Ch'ing Ming in spring and that of Chung Yeung in the late autumn. It is at the former that the bones are cleaned seven or ten years after burial. Both visits involve a meal sharing with the ancestors

and traditionally the pork was divided up between the male heirs ...

The dead can provide help but they can also create problems. If the living experience bad luck or worse it may be because they have neglected their duties to their ancestors. A young boy who died some years before may now desire a wife to keep him company in the world of the spirits. A spirit marriage is arranged with a family whose daughter has similarly died unmarried.

Inevitably there are the myriads of dead who have no living family to take care of their heeds and provide them with their portion on feast days. They are the Hungry Ghosts. On the seventh month they are let out of Hell to gather what scraps they can. At this time the entire community makes offerings of food and money in order to ward off the potential danger these ghosts pose.

Where do the dead reside? In Heaven? In Hell? In the Yellow Springs? In the air? In the rivers? In the earth? It depends on their status and on the believer. There is no single answer. They are everywhere.[72]

The worship of ancestors inevitably leads to spiritualistic practices—in an effort to communicate with the dead for the benefit of the living. Colonel Burkhardt, a longtime observer of Chinese society, writes principally of life in and around Hong Kong, but his observations are by no means limited to the Cantonese region or dialect:

Chinese constantly consult the spirits of their ancestors when embarking on a new venture, such as opening a business or building a house.

Where, however, the ancestral tablets are not available, owing for instance to absence from home, a medium is used to obtain contact. In this case it is essential to know the location of the grave of the person with whom it is desired to communicate.

Two sisters, employed as wash-amahs in different houses in Hong Kong, wished to get in touch with the spirit of their deceased mother, who is buried in a village near Kukong, up the North River from Canton. The journey is expensive and tedious, and letters are few and far between. The Communist censorship also takes any savour out of the gossip retailed. A third sister is working in Singapore but fails to answer letters. The idea was that a talk with the mother would clear up questions of the family welfare and solve the mystery of the sister's silence...

The medium closes her eyes, and joins her open hands with the finger tips touching and thumbs separate. This forms the 'Eight directions', in one of which every spirit in the universe is to be found. The first communication was startling, for the spirit replied that the mother was not available, as her father-in-law wished to speak with his grandchildren instead. Being of the senior generation he naturally had precedence, and no objection could be raised to his monopolizing the conversation...

Communication with the spirits has some resemblance to the 'over to you' of radiotelephony. The medium delivers the message to her clients, and then blows lightly into the tunnel of the Eight Directions to establish contact with the other world. As to the present conditions in the family, the grandfather stated that the Kitchen God was unhappy, the Door God disgruntled, and that even the Ancestral tablets found nothing to rejoice in. As attempts have been made to get them burned, and abolish all the old traditions in favour of pure materialism, there seems some justification in their apprehension.[73]

Tied to both ancestor worship and to polytheism is the propitiation of demons and evil spirits (the *kuei*). Kenneth Scott Latourette, who served as a missionary in China and later, at Yale, became the dean of American church historians, describes this belief in the following terms:

> In popular belief *kuei*—evil spirits or demons—are all about us and are of many kinds and shapes. They may have eyes on the tops of their heads.
>
> On occasion they may take the forms of animals or even of men and women. A *kuei* may be in a man-eating tiger. Great numbers of stories were told of animals—*kuei*—who could take at will the body of a man or especially of a beautiful woman and in that guise work harm. *Kuei* may be in old trees, or in clothes, in objects of furniture, or in mountains or stones. Leaves driven before the wind may each be a *kuei*. *Kuei* are responsible for all sorts of evils and misfortunes. They lurk in ponds and rivers to draw people in and drown them. Indeed, one theory had it that the *kuei* of a drowned person remains in the place of the tragedy and can obtain release only by luring some hapless Wight to a similar fate. The *kuei* of a mother who dies in childbirth, so it was believed, wins surcease from anguish by bringing on some other woman the same demise. Insane persons are controlled by *kuei*. An epidemic of *kuei* may visit a city—in the old days cutting queues and striking people on the streets. By committing suicide a man might, as a *kuei*, haunt the person whom he believed to have hounded him to the act. *Kuei* might be responsible for illnesses of various kinds. They might bring bad crops and famine.[74]

A seemingly milder form of divination ('white' as compared with 'black' magic) is fortune-telling. Its principal literary device, the *I-Ching*, has now become a dangerous object of veneration among Western occultists.[75] Latourette describes common divinatory practices which are still part of the Chinese folk religion:

> Each individual was supposed to have his fate in part determined by the year, month, day, and hour, or simply the year, month, and day, on which he was born. Each of these was indicated by a certain combination or one of the ten 'heavenly stems' and the twelve 'earthly branches'. The result was either eight or six characters which must be consulted by the fortune-teller in determining such matters as betrothals. There were lucky and unlucky days for marriages and funerals, for commencing building operations, or for beginning a journey. Among the many factors that could be taken into consideration in determining whether and when to enter upon a particular course of action were the five elements, the animals supposed to be identified with the twelve 'earthly branches', and combinations of the two, the calendar with its lucky and unlucky days (formerly published by imperial authority), the *pa kua* (eight trigrams) which form the basis of the *I Ching* and which from prehistoric times had been utilised by diviners, and the *I Ching* itself There were many ways of fortune-telling—among them the inspection of the physiognomy, the choice of a slip of paper by a bird and the interpretation of the picture or characters on the slip by the soothsayer, and the casting of lots by any one of several devices.[76]

Then there is the tree-worship component of traditional Chinese religion. Comments Burkhardt:

> It is unnecessary to go further than a mile from Tai Po to find an instance in every Hakka hamlet. Primitive man detected spirits in rocks, trees, and rivers, and, in spite of the shortage of fuel which has led to the deforestation of large areas of China, and impoverished the country through soil erosion, a prejudice persists against felling a large tree. In southern Fukien, their spirits are regarded as dangerous to offend. Many of the trees, however, are occupied by friendly spirits, who grant petitions, and are especially efficacious in case of sickness. These are garlanded with paper scrolls inscribed by grateful clients, or brightly coloured rags, accompanied by the same characters 'Honour the Spirit' which crown the reredos of the well altar. In one case a semicircle of rocks forms a sort of open-air chapel, whilst a large flat stone serves as altar. The incense burner bristled with half-burned red sticks, and two or three libation cups were a mute testimony to the generosity of the congregation.[77]

Finally, Chinese folk religion embraces beliefs and practices termed *fêng shui* (literally: wind and water). These also are by no means of uniquely historical interest:

> *Fêng shui* was based upon the belief that in every locality forces exist which act on graves, buildings, cities, and towns, either for the welfare or the ill of the quick and the dead. The object of *fêng shui*, therefore, was to discover the sites where the beneficent influences predominated, or so to alter, by artificial means, the surroundings of existing sites that the same happy results could be achieved. To attain these ends advice was sought from specialists in *fêng shui* . . .

> *Fêng shui* was especially used in determining the locations for interments. Stories abounded of families that had been mined because the grave of an ancestor had an unfavourable *fêng shui* and of others that prospered because of a fortunate location of ancestral remains. Whole cities, too, were said to have had their fortunes improved by the construction of a pagoda on expert advice.[78]

What is the significance of this superstitious popular religion in today's China? To be sure, it is far less influential in the cities than in the countryside, and the Marxist regime has done all within its power to root it out. But, ironically, folk religion has probably done more to help the autocratic reign of Deng's gerontocracy than it has hurt it. Latourette suggests a connection when he writes that Chinese folk beliefs

> may leave the impression that the religion of the majority was chaotic, uncritical, and an inconsistent jumble of beliefs and practices of varying origins. This is in part correct. Along with all the diversity, however, went a widespread feeling of unity—that the world, both seen and unseen, is after all a universe, and that there is one Power or Being who ultimately controls it and to whom appeal may be made. In the will of this One, conceived of as righteous, there was a good deal of quiet trust. This One was believed, in the long run, to even up the inequalities of life, in an individual or group, averaging the bitter with the sweet. For example, the High God of the people, known and revered all over China as *T'ien Lao Yeh, or Lao T'ien Fa Yeh*, or *Lao T'ien Yeh*, personalised Heaven, God, or Providence. Moreover, there was a good deal of determinism in the popular mind, *a kind of fatalism which bowed calmly to the*

> *inevitable, conceived of more or less dimly as the will of the inscrutable Power which governs the affairs of men.*[79]

In point of fact, the amorphous, theologically undefined, and essentially personal nature of Chinese folk religion offered no obstacle to centralised, totalitarian power; indeed, its fatalistic 'bowing to the inevitable' might even be said to encourage it. The Cult of Mao and his orthodox Marxist successors could well be understood, from such a viewpoint, as an earthly reflection of 'the inscrutable Power which governs the affairs of men'.

One can go deeper. Sociologist C. K. Yang has observed 'the organisational weakness of Chinese religions that helps to keep religion in a subordinate structural position among social institutions, thus preventing any successful attainment by religion of structural dominance'. He sees this weakness as

> rooted partly in the constant political suppression and control of religious organisations, and also possibly in some of the characteristics of Chinese religions, such as interfaith polytheism and magic.
>
> But perhaps the most important factor lies in the dominance of diffused religions in Chinese social life, since diffused religions possess no independent personnel and organisation of their own and are under the constant control of the secular leadership of social institutions into which they are diffused.[80]

'Interfaith polytheism and magic' does indeed constitute a 'diffused religion' incapable of any kind of organised, prophetic counterweight to political oppression. At best, folk religion may offer personal solace in a mysterious universe.

At worst, it bows to 'the constant control of the secular leadership', thereby allowing the latter to do whatever it wishes without religious reproach. We shall soon see that it is not only traditional folk religion in China that has taken this flaccid line of least resistance.

Taoism

Moving now to the classical religions of China, we begin with the oldest and the most related to traditional folk religion. Taoism takes its name from the *Tao* or universal principle, and appeared in the sixth century B.C., a century before the golden age of Greek philosophy.

The most important name in the early history of Taoism is that of its founder, Lao-tze, who can best be characterised as a mystic. (When we discuss Confucianism, we shall see how different in personality were Confucius, the practical moralist, and Lao-tze, the mystic.)

Little is known of the life of Lao-tze. The chief source of information is a 248-word biographical sketch written some five hundred years after the death of its subject—an interesting contrast with the life, death, and resurrection of Jesus Christ, all recounted by eyewitnesses testimony within little more than a generation of the events themselves.[81] In that biography of Lao-tze (by the 'Chinese Herodotus', Sma Chien), we are told that 'when he foresaw the decay of Chou, he departed and crossed the frontier'. One commentator has observed: 'Instead of resolutely facing the evils and attempting to apply his principle[s] concretely, as Confucius did, Lao-tze only talked some sage advice; and then he resigned from his government post into convenient irresponsibility, as many another Chinese official has done even to modern times.'[82] But by the eighth century A.D. he was canonised as the 'Great Sage Ancestor' and subsequently was made a member of the Taoist trinity.

The Taoist scriptures consist of a tractate attributed to Lao-tze, the *Tao-Teh-King*, for which, however, there is no evidence to link it to its supposed author. It has some remarkable parallels to the Bible (a German treatise by I. Hesse on 'Lao-tze: A Prechristian Witness to Truth' lists 268),[83] but it is so dry that the Emperor Ming Ti (third century A.D.) declared that punishment would come upon 'any official who either stretched, yawned, or expectorated' during his public reading of it. Another important Taoist holy writing is the later *Tai-Shang Kang-Ying Pien*. It contains high ethical sentiments, but also long lists of questionable moralistic trivia such as 'Don't listen to what your wife and concubines say'; 'Don't sing and dance on the last day of the month, or on the last day of the year'; 'Don't weep or spit toward the north'; 'Don't point at a rainbow'.

The heart of Taoism is the concept of the Tao itself. Etymologically, the word means 'Way', 'Path', 'Road'. In its highest sense, it designates the philosophical Absolute, the Supreme Being. It is sometimes rendered 'Reason' (i.e., the rational principle of the universe). In translating the Gospel of John into the Chinese, the *Logos*—the Word that was from the beginning with God and was God—is invariably rendered *Tao*.

Proper religious conduct is to live in accord with the *Tao*. But what does this mean? In the appendix to his *Abolition of Man*, C. S. Lewis uses the term to represent the sum total of the high moral teachings of the world's religions.[84] This, however, is not what the Taoist understands by *Tao*, indeed, the absence of any objective standard of morality in Taoism makes the distinguishing of good conduct from bad largely a subjective affair. The most common ethical phrase in Taoism is *wu-wei*, which translates as 'non-striving', 'doing nothing', 'inactivity'. Dutch ambassador, polymath, sinologist, and mystery writer Robert Van Gulik translates a poem of Ch'ang-tzu (fourth century B.C.) on the subject as follows:

> You can't say Tao exists
> You can't say Tao does not exist
> But you can find it in the silence,
> in *wu-wei* (deedlessness).[85]

The idea may be, as has been suggested by some interpreters, that perfect conduct consists of placid contentment—a sublime indifference toward everything and everybody, even as Aristotle's Supreme Being contemplated only himself, thereby avoiding all other concerns which would necessarily disturb his perfection. If so, it stands 180 degrees removed from Christianity, where God, seeing the human race dead in trespasses and sins, so loved us that he came to earth to die for our miseries and raise us to glory: the very antithesis of 'inactivity'. But the undefined vagueness of the concept opens it up to a plethora of interpretations, certainly justifying ethical indifferentism. Without a '*Tao* made flesh'—to give personal and revelational substance to metaphysical and ethical ideals—one is left in a never-never land of ambiguity and amorality.

And, in fact, this has been the sad modern history of the Taoist movement. In practice, Taoism has taken on most of the worst features of Chinese folk religion as discussed earlier. Thus Hume:

> The actual outworkings of the system have been quite different from the high theories of its founder. Yet the Tao-Teh-King itself presents some basis for all of the later developments of Taoism except the hierarchical papacy. Taoists have lost almost totally their founder's original protest against social disorders and his measure of ethical idealism. Taoism has always been mystical, but through most of its history it has interpreted the mysterious mostly in magical and anti-scientific terms. Taoism presents a

> pathetic history. It started with some admirable features, but it has degraded fearfully into polytheism, demonolatry, witchcraft, and occultism . . .
>
> The social morality of the Taoist priests is in general ill repute. The easiest approximation to the unperturbed condition of the immortal Tao is now conceived to be accomplished through the method of retiring into a monastery or a nunnery, and there living inactively so as to produce prodigious longevity. Every one of the authorities who deals with Taoism from personal knowledge of it, utters condemnation.[86]

Taoism blends with Chinese folk religion ideologically in its use of the traditional categories of the *Yin* and the *Yang*—the male and female principles that represent the perpetual interaction of opposites in the universe. This constantly unfolding flux of *Yin* and *Yang* characterises both the uncreated macrocosmic universe and the microcosmic world of the human body. In Needham's phrase, the Taoist cosmos is 'the web that has no weaver'.[87] A third century B.C. Taoist philosopher put it this way:

> The operations of Heaven are profoundly mysterious. It has water-levels for levelling, but it does not use them; it has plumblines for setting things upright, but it does not use them. It works in deep stillness . . .
>
> Thus it is said. Heaven has no form and yet the myriad things are brought to perfection. It is like the most impalpable of featureless essences, and yet the myriad changes are all brought about by it. So also the sage is busied about nothing, and yet the thousand executives of State are effective in the highest degrees.

> This may be called the untaught teaching, and the wordless edit.

Comments Kaptchuk on this passage, in his effort to understand and to evaluate Chinese medicine:

> The Chinese description of reality does not penetrate to a truth; it can only be a poetic description of a truth that cannot be grasped ... For the Chinese, this description of the eternal process of Yin and Yang is the only way to try to explain either the workings of the universe or the workings of the human body. And it is enough, because the process is all there is; no underlying truth is ever within reach. The truth is imminent in everything and is the process itself ...
>
> New ideas in Western science, ideas that point toward an awareness of the totality of being, have arisen as a direct result of the Western urge to penetrate phenomena and to find the transcendent truth behind them. Western thought, at its most noble and honest, is nourished by the constant tension between unknown and known, imperfect and perfect. Western humanity is quickened by a metaphysical dilemma—on the one hand, it was created in the image of the Almighty, and on the other, it was created from dust. Western humankind is enmeshed in creating and becoming; it labours in growth and development. Perhaps this is a consequence of Judeo-Christian emphasis on an omnipresent, transcendent God making impossible the attainment of human perfection ... In any case it is an idea altogether missing in China.[88]

Confucianism

The second of the officially recognized *San Chiao* or classical 'Three Religions' of China is Confucianism. It appeared shortly after the beginnings of Taoism; indeed, Confucius and Lao-tze were contemporaries.

There is no better way to understand the difference in style and approach of these two religions than to listen to the encounter Confucius had with Lao-tze when the former, at age thirty-four, visited the latter owing to his official position as archivist at the court of the dynasty of Chou and his reputation as the 'Venerable Philosopher'.

> Lao-tze chided that historian-to-be and busy young reformer, who desired to search out the ancient history of China and to restore its passing glory by a scheme of social proprieties.
>
>> 'The men about whom you talk are dead, and their bones are mouldered to dust. Put away your proud airs and many desires.'
>
> Instead, Lao-tze urged Confucius to search quietly and personally for the Tao, which is the mystic principle of the universe, and which alone can furnish the key to religion and life. When the young man asserted that he had been studying diligently in books for twenty years past, Lao-tze replied:
>
>> 'If the Tao could be offered to men, who would not wish to offer it to his Prince? If it could be presented to men, who would not wish to present it to his parents? If it could be announced to men, who would not wish to announce it to his brethren? If it could be transmitted to men, who would not wish to

transmit it to his children? Why do you not obtain it? This is the reason: Because you do not give it an asylum in your heart.'

After this interview Confucius, who later was to be recognized as the most famous scholar and teacher of all China, said to his disciples:

'I know how the birds fly, how the fishes swim, how animals run. But there is the Dragon. I cannot tell how it mounts on the wind through the clouds, and flies through Heaven. To-day I have seen Lao-tze, and I can only compare him to the Dragon [i.e., supra-mundane and unintelligible mystery].'

Lao-tze must have appeared to Confucius like another-worldly dreamer, soaring among the clouds of his own speculations. And Confucius must have seemed to Lao-tze like a busybody, meddling in everybody's affairs. The two most influential men of China were indeed different from one another in their interests, aims, methods, and general systems.[89]

Confucius spent his life as a teacher (the private school he started reached an enrolment of three thousand students) and as a state official (ultimately becoming a chief justice). He devoted his final years to editing and writing works which became the sacred scriptures of Confucianism— though he never claimed any kind of divine inspiration for them. These include the Canonical Classics (one of which is the *I-Ching*, referred to earlier in our discussion of Chinese folk religion), and the Four Books, most notable of which are the *Analects* (Confucius' collected sayings) and the works of Mencius, Confucius' great disciple and expositor.

Some have argued that Confucianism should not be treated as a religion at all, but rather as a philosophy. True, Confucius was indifferent to metaphysical questions, and did not concern himself at all with the issues of God's existence or the worship of him. 'While you cannot serve men,' he answered an inquirer, 'how can you serve spirits?' When the same inquirer asked about life after death, he received a similar reply: 'While you do not know life, what can you know about death?' (*Analects* ix. 11:1). However, the final section of the *Analects*[90] contains such passages as 'The Master said, "Without recognising the ordinances of Heaven it is impossible to be a superior man,"' and ultimately the veneration and temple worship of Confucius himself (including extensive animal sacrifice) became an integral part of the imperial state religion. In the name of Confucianism, government officials during the empire served as priests of Heaven, conducting what amounted to nature-worship. And the practice of ancestor worship, which we have seen to be one of the most important elements in Chinese folk religion, became central to Confucianism through its emphasis on filial piety.

But what was the core of Confucius' own teaching? Y. C. Yang has said that 'Confucianism is a one-word religion.'[91] The word he refers to is *Jen*, a composite character made up of the two simple characters *man* and *the number two*. The idea here is that a person is never alone, for there is always a 'second man' to be taken into account. If the underlying powerful Christian theology were to be removed from John Donne's famous aphorism, much the same would be

> conveyed in—his words: 'No man is an island unto himself.' Probably the best translation of *Jen* is simply 'altruism'.

And here we arrive at Confucius' ethic of *Shu* or 'reciprocity', and his famous negative statement of the Golden Rule: 'What you do not want done to yourself do not to others' (*Analects*, xv. 23). This so-called 'Silver Rule' (not Golden because it is framed negatively) was put in more positive terms by Confucius' disciple Mencius when he exhorted his followers to 'treat with due consideration and regard the aged ones of our own and extend the same to the aged of others; in the same way, treat the younger ones of our own and extend the same to the younger ones of others' (*Mencius*, Bk. I, Pt. I, vii. 12).

Since this altruistic principle of reciprocity has no theological underpinnings, it really functions as little more than a philosophical or ethical proposal. When Confucius says, 'If this is where you would like to stand, then let him stand here also' (*Analects*, vi. 23:2), one thinks inevitably of Kant's categorical imperative: 'So act that your action may become a universal rule.' But, as I have argued elsewhere:

> The reply of the thoroughly self-centred person, the fanatic, the revolutionary, or the anarchist may well be: 'I'll act without regard for others (or the other side) if I can get away with it.' Experientially, we all know that others do not or cannot always give the actor tit for tat, so in the absence of a final accounting (a Last Judgement) the unprincipled person may well choose to disregard the rights of others when he has the power to get away with it. The condottieri of Machiavelli's time, Burkhardt tells us, enjoyed the game of rolling boulders from their castles down onto their peasants working in the fields; since they

feared neither God nor man, they did what pleased them, in total disregard of any principle of universalisation. Human rights violations of our day have the same shape, and the violators continue to say, 'So what?'[92]

That which a critic wrote of Kant could apply equally to Confucius:

In the end, we must conclude that Kant failed to discover a way to deduce objective, obligatory ends from the mere analysis of what it is to be a rational agent. He was therefore unable also to establish the unconditionally universal validity of any substantive principles of practical reason.[93]

Is it any wonder that the Confucian ethic has done little to restrain imperial autocracy through Chinese history or the present-day manifestations of centralised governmental power in that land?

Confucianism has maintained unflappable confidence in human nature. True, the third century B.C. Confucian philosopher Hsün Tzu asserted that some men were 'incorrigibly evil' and in general had a low view of man. But though he has been called 'the moulder of ancient Confucianism', Hsün Tzu's views in this respect did not prevail.[94] Confucius himself was convinced that men are perfectible through education. (Sadly, Confucius never had Plato's experience. After writing of the ideal 'philosopher-king' in *The Republic*, Plato had the opportunity to educate the prince of Syracuse, who turned out to be a dunderhead. Plato then revised his previous view that a sovereign should stand above the law.)

Of what, specifically, does the Confucian educative process consist? What particular virtues are to be inculcated? Professor Yang sets these forth with admirable clarity:

While *Jen* is declared to be the root and measure of all virtues in human relations, in order to be more explicit and specific we have laid down for us the five cardinal virtues to which we should particularly pay attention. These are *Jen* or Benevolence, *Yi* or Righteousness, *Li* or Propriety, *Chih* or Wisdom, and *Hsin* or Fidelity, that is, faith and faithfulness. The first three belong to the realm of theory, and the second two belong to the realm of action. The first three are objects to be comprehended, and the second two are objects to be demonstrated or practised in conduct.

The relationship of the first three can perhaps be best explained by using a tree as an analogy. *Jen* or Benevolence (in the larger Confucian sense) is the root of all moral, good and proper, action. *Yi* or Righteousness is the trunk of the tree, the manifestations of *Jen* in its applications to life and living. *Li* or rules of Propriety (including etiquette and ceremony but larger than both) are the various branches of the trunk, or the concrete detailed rules of conduct based upon the idea of Righteousness which springs from Benevolence (comparable to the laws of the Pharisees). *Chih* or Wisdom is the apprehension of Truth. *Hsin* or Fidelity is faith and faithfulness in the application of the knowledge of Truth thus apprehended. If we should continue further the use of the figure of the tree, we could say that Wisdom is the flower, and Faith the fruit, on this tree of virtue.

Confucianism recognizes five fundamental relations in society. These are those between sovereign and minister (or between the state and the citizen), between father and son, between husband and wife, between elder brother and younger brother, and between friends. Between father and son there should be family affection; between sovereign and minister, righteousness; between husband and wife, differentiation of functions (or division of labour); between elder brother and younger brother, a proper order of precedence; between friends, fidelity . . .

These five fundamental relations involve ten different parties, giving rise to ten different principles or attitudes which, by analogy, may be called the 'ten commandments of Confucian philosophy'. These ten principles, as stated in the classics, are that the father should be kind; the son, filial; the elder brother, good; the younger brother, respectful, the husband, righteous; the wife, listening; the elder, gracious; the junior, complaisant; the ruler or king, benevolent (*Jen*); the subjects or officials, loyal.[95]

The Confucian social ethic is based on an underlying philosophy of the body politic. Just as Confucius assumed that the universe was fundamentally harmonious (he had no conception of a fallen world) and that man was basically good (for him, sin had no meaning at all), so Confucianism's social principles assume a stable, hierarchically organised society.

The ethics of Confucianism are the ethics of a dignified aristocracy which prided itself on a long-established social order, and which despised outlandish barbarians. No other ethical system in the world has so emphatically prescribed to rulers duties for the welfare of the people in the state. The ethics of Confucianism were clearly formulated in an age self-contained and self-satisfied. They do not contain provisions for problems of industrialism, democracy, and internationalism.[96]

True, Munro has tried to argue for a fundamental egalitarianism in Confucian thought, claiming that 'previous commentators on classical Chinese philosophy have been misled by the Confucian assertion that a hierarchical society is justified by the hierarchical character of nature itself, and that men are of unequal merit'.[97] But even he only attempts to show (minimalistically) that Confucianism believed all men *at birth* shared common attributes; he does not even try to disprove the overwhelmingly well established fact that for Confucians *adults* are of unequal merit and cannot therefore legitimately claim equal treatment economically or politically. Even if Munro is right that Confucianism held to a form of 'natural equality', this is of little practical importance, for social structures inevitably mould us in different and unequal ways as we grow up and Confucianism tells us that we are to subordinate ourselves to those structures, since they represent the will of Heaven.

Professor Yang states flatly that the Confucian social ethic deals with 'duties and obligations, and not rights and interests'.[98] Confucianism nowhere addresses the civil and political liberties of the subject: rather, all emphasis is placed on the duty of the ruler to treat the subject fairly. But suppose he doesn't? The subject's duty is to obey the sovereign, and he is in no position to insist upon his rights (which, in any case, are left undefined—indeed undiscussed). It should be painfully clear that such a philosophy easily justifies autocratic rule, and can hardly be appealed to in opposition to totalitarian affronts to human dignity.

And without an eternal reference point for the value of the human being and his God-given rights, what could we expect? James Legge of Oxford, perhaps the greatest nineteenth-century English authority on Chinese thought in general and Confucianism in particular, concluded his analysis of Confucius' teachings with these sobering words:

His teaching was thus hardly more than a pure secularism. He had faith in man, man made for society, but he did not care to follow him out of society, nor to present to him motives of conduct derived from the consideration of a future state. Good and evil would be recompensed by the natural issues of conduct within the sphere of time,—if not in the person of the actor, yet in the persons of his descendants. If there were any joys of heaven to reward virtue, or terrors of future retribution to punish vice, the sage took no heed of the one or the other. Confucius never appeared to give the evils of polygamy a thought. He mourned deeply the death of his mother; but no generous word ever passed his lips about woman as woman. Nor had he the idea of any progress or regeneration of society. The stars all shone to him in the same heavens behind; none beckoned brightly before. It was no doubt the moral element of his teaching, springing out of his view of human nature, which attracted many of his disciples, and still holds the best part of the Chinese men of learning bound to him; but the conservative tendency of his lessons . . . is the chief reason why successive dynasties have delighted to do him honour.[99]

Buddhism

The third of the classic 'Three Religions' of China originated in India but reached China about A.D. 70, contemporaneously with the destruction of Jerusalem at the hands of the Romans. Buddhism became thoroughly acclimated to Chinese civilisation and its temples are found everywhere; in our first chapter we spoke of our visit to the Wild Goose Pagoda, a very famous Buddhist temple, in Xian. All varieties of Buddhism are represented in China, though Mahayana

Buddhism predominates. There are some ten Buddhist sects in the country; two are Hinayana and the other eight belong to the Mahayana school, and among the Mahayana variety are representatives of both Pure Land Buddhism and Zen.

The founder of Buddhism, Gautama (his Sanscrit name) is supposed to have lived from 560 to 480 B.C. But accurate historical facts about him are virtually nonexistent. In the definitive modern life of Buddha we are told that 'in the present state of our knowledge we cannot in any instance declare that Buddha said so and so. The fact that we start from is that we have a collection of documents, which were held some two centuries after Buddha to contain his utterances.'[100] The most striking event in these questionable accounts of his life is the story of his so-called 'Great Renunciation' at the age of twenty-nine.

> While out pleasure driving Prince Gautama was deeply impressed by four passing sights, viz.: a decrepit old man, a loathsomely sick man, a corpse, and a calm religious ascetic unperturbed by any suffering. He became distressed at the thought that he himself and all mankind were liable to the miseries of oncoming old age, sickness, and death. And he became convinced that only resolute self-sacrifice and search would win triumphant peace. Therefore, despite a fierce temptation, he renounced his wife, a new-born son, and the inheritance of his father's throne. Cutting off his hair, he assumed the garb of a monk.[101]

Upon recognising what philosophers have come to term the 'human predicament', Gautama endeavoured to find a solution for it. He followed the Hindu path of metaphysical speculation and the Jainist route of bodily asceticism, but found no peace. Finally, one night, while sitting cross-legged under a *bo*-tree (the tree subsequently became the prime object of Buddhist pilgrimage), he arrived at enlightenment (in Sanscrit, *buddha*, Gautama's name from that point on). Enlightenment came through his discovery of the 'Four Noble Truths' and the 'Noble Eightfold Path', by the application of which one could be freed from the burden of *karma* or guilt which necessitated continual rebirths (the Hindu doctrine of the transmigration of souls) and enter the blissful state of Nirvana or non-existence— 'as the candle's flame is reabsorbed into the sun and as the droplet of rain re-enters the ocean whence it came'.

The Four Noble Truths are: (1) All existence is suffering; (2) Desire is the cause of suffering; (3) All suffering will therefore cease when we suppress all desires; (4) To eliminate desire one must adhere to the Noble Eightfold Path. The Noble Eightfold Path, in turn, consists of right belief, aspiration, speech, action, livelihood, endeavour, thought, and concentration.

Buddha spent the remainder of his long life in preaching this message and in making and training disciples. After his death he was first venerated and later deified. The Mahayana ('Greater Vehicle') branch of Buddhism ultimately declared that when Gautama delayed his entrance into Nirvana after enlightenment, he did it as an essential model: the *bodhisattva* (enlightened disciple) will compassionately refuse the state of full blessedness until others are led into that state as well. The 'Pure Land' variant of Mahayana Buddhism is often said to proclaim salvation by grace through faith.

But these seeming parallels to Christianity are only skin deep. Sparks notes that Buddhism and Christianity relate history to eternity in two different, incompatible ways: 'Whereas Buddha "enters" history to exhibit compassion and to reveal a saving truth which is independent of history, Christ "enters" history in order to accomplish and confirm by his death and resurrection a salvation which is incomplete without such historical involvement.'[102]

Last photos from Tiananmen Square (2 June 1989).

Soldiers exercising before the Massacre.

Protest parades in Xian following the Massacre.

Through protesting demonstrators to the Xian Airport, Monday 5 June 1989.

The Author with Pastor Bao Jia-quan at the Nanjing Union Theological Seminary.

The Author with General Manager, Peter MacInnis in Nanjing.

Symbolic funeral procession in Nanjing remembering those slaughtered in Tiananmen Square.

Christian Art Class at the Nanjing Union Theological Seminary.

As for the Buddhist sect of Pure Land (known in Japan as Jodo and Jodo Shin-shu), the claim is that salvation allegedly attained by complete commitment to the grace of Amida-Buddha is equivalent to the central Christian doctrine of salvation by grace through faith in Jesus Christ. Nothing could be further from the truth. Let us hear from three specialists on the question.

Fumio Masutani, professor at the Tokyo University of Foreign Studies and himself a Pure Land Buddhist, asserts:

> Fundamentally speaking, Buddha is the ideal which man aims to attain . . . It is undeniable that there is a fundamental difference between Christianity and Buddhism. Buddhism starts with the idea that man is an existence, while Christianity says that man is a creature. Christianity teaches that in the very beginning, there was God from whom all things are derived and that this God is the fundamental fact and not merely a simile or an expedient. On the other hand, Amida Buddha is more or less in the nature of an expedient (*ooben-setsu*) because it is made by the consciousness, that is, it is a creation of the mind (*ishiki-shozo no mono*).[103]

Steinilber-Oberlin interviewed several bonzes of the Pure Land persuasion.

> What essential difference do you see between your doctrine and Christianity, which also comprises a Saviour, a Paradise and only requires of men— Faith? I asked curiously. 'In Christianity, God is all, man is nothing. According to the Jodo and Shinsu sects, man escapes from suffering and reaches the supreme goal, not, it is true, by his own merit, which is too weak, but thanks to the compassionate

intervention of Buddha. But Buddha is a man. As I was saying to you a moment ago, Amida-Buddha can be compared to lunar light. This light is everywhere present, *but it only exists for those who look at it. If humanity did not exist, Amida-Buddha would not exist either.* Amida-Buddha exists in function to human life, and his beneficent activity is in function of men's desire to reach a refuge—salvation. In Christianity everything goes from God to man; the two terms apply to two entirely difference personalities, the one being the creature of the other. The one is All—the other nothing. In the Jodo and Shin doctrines *a human ascent towards the Pure Land takes place.* We all become Buddha, and we are so already in a certain degree, since Amida-Buddha is space, Time, Eternal Life' . . .

I next asked the two bonzes [Kenryo Kawasaki and Fujioka of the Shinshu sect] the question I had previously asked the bonze Kanei Okamoto, of the Jodo sect. 'Since, according to your sect, Buddhism exacts from the believer faith in an adored Saviour, what essential difference do you establish between Christianity and your doctrine?' I received the same answer—i.e. that Buddhism does not recognize any omnipotent God exterior to the creature, to whom He dictates his duties. *Buddhism is exclusively a human, moral and philosophical system.* Amida-Buddha, the Saviour, is in function with humanity which needs to be saved. And Mr. Fujioka resumed this in the following impressive formula: '*It is not because there is a Buddha that Humanity exists. It is because Humanity exists that there is a Buddha.*'[104]

Callaway, in a doctoral dissertation involving extensive research in printed sources (50 pages of notes) and interviews with Japanese Buddhist leaders, shows that Pure Land Buddhism actually reduces to monistic idealism:

> When considered in terms of *hooben* [a teaching device, an accommodation to language; Sanskrit: *upaya*], Shin seems theistic . . . It should be noted, however, that even when set forth in terms of personality, there are fundamental differences between the concept of *Amida* and that of the Heavenly Father of Christianity. For instance, when viewed realistically, Amida must be conceived as a human being who attained his divinity by his own efforts . . . Amida is, after all, like all other particular entities—merely a thought-image in, the *busshin* [the ultimate Buddha Reality]. . . . The *Shin* concept of Amida seems theistic only when superficially viewed. Ultimately, *Shin* is pantheistic . . . Ultimately, *Shin* is atheistic in the same sense that Zen is atheistic. The Absolute with which both sects are concerned is the same. Amida and the *busshin* are one . . . To seek Amida beyond the empirical self is, after all, no different from seeking the *busshin* within. The quest of *Shin* and the quest of Zen differ only in terminology, not in fact.[105]

The sacred scriptures of Buddhism consist of the Tripitaka (the 'Three Baskets' of Wisdom—the Discipline Basket, the Teaching Basket, and the Metaphysical Basket or Higher Doctrine) in the Pali dialect, together with a large body of non-canonical, traditional literature in Sanskrit. The Tripitaka itself consists of some ten thousand pages, and only part of it has been translated into other languages, including Chinese. Some of the most fetching literature of China (such as the tales of Monkey) recount the partly historical, partly imaginary travels of Buddhist monies who bring scripture from India to China. Yet

> the canonical scriptures of Buddhism contain no complete biography of the founder, no report of any later leader continuing the work of the founder, no historic application of the highest Buddhist principles to the regeneration of society, no intimation of a creative purpose or power in the world, and no prophetic vision of a glorious abundant life here or hereafter.[106]

Why is there 'no application of the highest Buddhist principles to the regeneration of society'? The answer is that at its very heart Buddhism takes its adherent away from society. In the final analysis, all is *maya* (illusion). Professor Yang characterises Buddhism as 'the path of escape', and observes that, 'to the Buddhist the world is purely subjective. To him there is no objective reality in the outside world. Life is but a dream; the world is but a make-believe phenomenon.'[107] The object of personal existence is to separate oneself from all desire—including a desire to alter the nature of society—so as to avoid the round of transmigrations/reincarnations and pass from this illusory world of phenomena into the blissful non-existence of Nirvana. Quite obviously such a world-view, even if one leaves aside its analytic, epistemological meaninglessness,[108] is utterly incapable of responding to questions of social justice. Hume, after quoting the standard Buddhist aphorism, 'Let him [the disciple] wander alone like a rhinoceros', makes the devastating but accurate judgement: 'The main trend in Buddhist ethics is negative, repressive, quietistic, individualistic, anti-social.'[109]

Indeed, it may well be asked whether Buddhism has any defined ethic at all. After a frustrating decade in Marxism, novelist Arthur Koestler went on a year's pilgrimage to drink at the founts of Buddhist wisdom. He founds gurus whose messages were totally ambiguous and Zen monks who had had no difficulty in volunteering as kamikaze pilots.[110]

Koestler concluded that the absence of any objective standards of right and wrong in Buddhism makes the religion a social liability. This is of course particularly the case when, as in Tiananmen Square, good and evil meet each other head on, and the interests of justice cry out for support and principled commitment.

Some Concluding Generalisations

Latourette, speaking of the overall Chinese religious scene, notes what he calls 'a kind of slovenliness in the temples and in the carrying out of the ceremonies'. Our first-hand contact with Chinese life in June of 1989, twenty-five years after Latourette wrote on the subject, brought us to exactly the same conclusion.

> Even before the anti-religious wave of the 1920s and after, a large proportion of the temples seemed to be in a state of chronic neglect, and a visit between important occasions would often find courts weed-grown and the great halls dusty and festooned with cobwebs. While ceremonies were supposed to conform to prescribed forms, and correct posturing, costuming, and utterances of phrases were emphasized, yet, as in the case of funerals when beggars were employed to fill out the procession, the wearers of the elaborate clothing might be unwashed, and in the less obvious corners of the shrine dust and debris might lie undisturbed.[111]

'Chronic neglect' as a characteristic of Chinese religion certainly reflects the efforts of Marxism and particularly its cultural revolution to extirpate the 'opium of the people'. But it is also a commentary on the debility both of Chinese folk religion and of the three classical Chinese faiths to meet the deepest needs of the people.

Tiananmen Square is a symbol of the inevitable confrontation between autocratic, dictatorial, totalitarian power and the perennial longings of the citizenry for civil rights, freedom of communication, and government free from nepotism and corruption. But what does Chinese religion offer in this conflict? Ironically, it aligns itself much more naturally with the Marxist leadership that would eliminate it than it does with the protesters of 3–4 June!

Chinese folk religion totally neglects social justice in its preoccupation with the superstitious satisfaction of personal and familial needs. Taoism and Confucianism have always allied themselves with the aristocratic, autocratic, imperial status quo. Buddhism's unworldliness offers no opposition whatever to social evils in general or to totalitarianism in particular.

> One last general characteristic of Chinese religion that needs mention is state control. As far back as the Chou and probably earlier, religion was a function of society as expressed in such institutions as the state and the family. When, under the Ch'in, the Empire was organised, the authority of the state in religion was rigorously exercised. In theory the state remained supreme in such matters down through the Ch'ing. The control of the state was not always vigorously asserted. A good deal of practical toleration existed. Yet the right was always there and from time to time was emphatically exercised. No great religious organisation has ever made an effective bid for superiority over the state in the loyalties of the Chinese.[112]

But by far the greatest single weakness of Chinese religion vis-à-vis societal needs—and the chief source of its ethical slovenliness and flaccidity—is its absence of any clearly defined, justifiable standards of personal and social ethics.

Whether one looks at the impossibly vague *Tao* and the deedless *wu-wei* of Taoism, or at the naive altruism and formalistic categorical imperative of Confucianism, or at the escapism and ethical simple-mindedness of much of Buddhist thought (the Eightfold Path, for example, has a compelling force roughly equivalent to that of the Boy Scout Law), one is not surprised at the inability of these viewpoints to present any meaningful case for human rights or against a leadership that would slaughter unarmed student protesters.

Moreover, not one of these traditional or classic religions provides a way to change the heart so as to arrive at genuine concern for one's fellow man. All of Chinese religion either considers man basically good and not requiring redemption (folk religion, Taoism, Confucianism) or sees him capable of saving himself through a consciously chosen renunciation of both the world in which he lives and the people with whom he has contact (Buddhism). Another route entirely must be sought if China is to rise above its autocratic past, a past which is reflected as much today in Deng's gerontocracy as in the imperial dynasties of yesterday.

CHAPTER FIVE

THE CHURCH IN CHINA: IS THERE A GOSPEL ANSWER?

*T*he current 'official' religion of China—Marxism—together with the folk and classical religions of that land—have been weighed in the balance and found wanting. At best, none of them has offered appropriate resistance to totalitarian human-rights violations by the controlling regime; at worst, they have aided and abetted these violations by their blind acceptance of centralised political authority or indifference to social conditions in this world. Now, however, we shall examine a religious answer of a very different kind.

But why look to religion at all, especially in light of the failures of such highly regarded faiths as Taoism, Confucianism, and Buddhism? The fact of the matter is that we have no choice; without a solid transcendental standard of social ethics, no basis at all exists for declaring the Tiananmen Square massacre evil or for opposing those who perpetrated it.

The founder of the analytical philosophy movement, Ludwig Wittgenstein, in his *Tractatus Logico-Philosophicus*, demonstrated logically that 'the sense of the world must lie outside the world' (6:41), that is, man never has sufficient perspective from within the world situation to build an absolute structure of truth and value: absolute truth and eternal value, if they exist at all, must take their origin from outside the flux of the human situation. More recently, Kurt

Baier, one of the foremost ethical thinkers to benefit from Wittgensteinian insights, has admitted that from within the human situation ethical values can never rise above the societal level: 'Outside society, the very distinction between right and wrong vanishes.'[113] Human beings, in other words, are incapable of reaching absolute ethical norms by unaided reason: their ethic will always reflect their stance in society. As Wittgenstein put it in the *Tractatus*: 'If there is any value that does have value, it must lie outside the whole sphere of what happens and is the case . . . Ethics is transcendental' (6.41–6.421).'[114]

The plain consequence is that the only possible route to absolute ethical standards and inalienable rights would have to lie in a revelation from outside the world. If such a revelation does not exist, man will of logical (not merely practical) necessity remain forever bound to his cultural relativities, forever incapable of establishing a true standard of human worth.

In his Nobel lecture, Solzhenitsyn posed a series of questions that existentially display the acute need for revelational aid in the sphere of human rights.

> Who is going to create for all mankind one single system of values for evil deeds and good deeds, for what is intolerable and what is tolerable, and where the boundary between them lies today? Who will make clear for mankind what is really unbearable and heinous and what, because of its nearness to us, is only a scratch on the skin—and, thus, direct our wrath against what is really terrible, and not merely something close to us? Who might be capable of communicating such understanding across the barrier of personal human experience? Who might possibly be able to instill in the narrow, stubborn human essence the grief and joy of others

who are far away, a perception of a range of facts and delusions which they have never experienced themselves?[115]

Clearly, the only meaningful answer to these questions would be a transcendent Deity—a living, personal God who would revelationally impart his standards of human dignity to man and soteriologically enter human hearts to change indifference and hatred to concern and love. This is precisely the claim of biblical Christianity: 'God was in Christ, reconciling the world unto Himself.'

As compared with *Marxism*, Christian faith realistically locates selfishness (sin) in *all* men, not just in a privileged class of capitalists, and provides the solution of a transformed heart rather than a superficial, external alteration in the ownership of the means of production in society. The Christian standard of human rights is absolute and inalienable, resting in God's objective biblical declarations to mankind, not subject to the shifting sands of Party leadership or material-economic conditions.

Unlike the magical and occult world-view of *traditional Chinese folk religion*, Christianity recognises that man cannot manipulate the cosmos to achieve ultimate happiness. That was the error of the builders of the Tower of Babel and of King Saul when he consulted the witch of Endor. Rather, one must begin with the recognition that such techniques are a reflection of the problem, not a means to its solution. Mankind's problem is that in its self-centredness it tries to play God. The true answer is to give up all attempts at self-salvation and accept God's gracious gift of himself in Christ, thereby becoming a 'new creature' from' the inside out.

Christianity offers what *Taoism* seeks but can never find within its religious framework: a clear understanding of the *Tao*—indeed, the '*Tao* made flesh', appearing in our midst and dying to restore us to true harmony with the universe.

Christ the Word sets forth objective moral standards, not a vacuous 'deedlessness', and thus provides a solid basis for opposing the inhumanity of autocratic political power.

The biblical message sees man for what he is: not the *Confucian* ideal of inherent goodness capable of perfection through education, but a fallen creature who, again and again through history, has destroyed his fellow man when he can get away with it. Christianity insists that mankind needs redemption, not just education, and that the loftiest ethical ideals mean little until the heart is changed so that these ideals are interiorised and a person's motivations become Christlike.

In stark contrast with *Buddhism*'s refusal to see the phenomenal world as reality, the Christian religion declares that this world was real enough that God himself, out of love for us, willingly entered it and subjected himself to all its terrors and miseries for our salvation. And if our world was that real to our God and Saviour, it is real enough for us to take it seriously and do all within our power to oppose the evils in it and strive for justice and human rights for our fellow creatures. We have no justification to 'escape' from the world of political and social reality—and instead of trying to 'eliminate desire', we are to distinguish the desire for evil from the desire for good and do all within our power to maximise the good. The Christian Scriptures, moreover, define what is good in concrete terms: not 'the sound of one hand clapping' of the Zen koan, but the command to 'love as Christ loved us' of the New Testament.

In sum, the failure of the philosophical and religious options discussed in preceding chapters must not keep us from considering-a different ultimate solution altogether. If Christianity is true (and we shall have something to say on that score before concluding our discussion), it can offer an unparalleled analytical tool for comprehending the current Chinese situation and aiding its future development.

Christian Missions in China

But if the Christian message is genuinely capable of doing something for today's China, why has it apparently done so little for that land in the past? Here we need to look at the history of Christian missionary endeavour in China as background to the needs of today.[116]

Well before Marco Polo's famous visit to China (1288), Nestorian Christians brought the gospel to that land. These earliest missionaries to China were of Semitic extraction and came from the Mesopotamian region. They were not in doctrinal fellowship with either the Eastern (Greek) or the Western (Roman) church, for they followed the monothelite views of their founder Nestorius (fifth century).[117]

But the unique elements in the Nestorians' christological position were so obscure as to have little or no practical effect on their evangelism. The problem with Nestorian missionary work in China came from a different quarter. In their laudable effort to 'become all things to all men that by all means some might be saved', they clothed the Christian message in Confucian thought-forms. Unfortunately, they did not restrict themselves to using Confucian teachings as a point of departure and common ground; they went on to absorb Confucian—and even Buddhist—ideas into their theology. Thus, for example, they allowed communication with dead ancestors as practised in the mix of Chinese folk religion and the classical faiths to blend with prayers for the dead, purgatory, and other related beliefs of medieval Christendom. Fascinatingly enough, Nestorianism survives even today among a few Mongols on China's northern border.

The Nestorian lesson is certainly that, even with all the good will in the world and the best of motives, one must guard tenaciously against weakening the deposit of faith by accepting into it unbeliever ideas that contradict its substance. Indeed, this has been the great error of liberal

Christianity in modern times: in the naive belief that the unbeliever will only come to the faith if we conform the faith to his ideas, the liberal denatures the faith once delivered to the saints until it no longer represents Christianity at all! Such an approach leaves the unbeliever with no saving message, so if he does accept the new 'Christianity' he actually acquires a powerless non-gospel that does him little good.

In the thirteenth century the Polo brothers returned to the West with an invitation from the Kublai Khan to the Pope for 'one hundred teachers of learning and religion'. The great Khan declared:

> So shall I be baptised, and when I am baptised, all my barons and lords will be baptised, and their subjects will receive baptism, and so there will be more Christians here than in your own country.[118]

Franciscan missionaries responded to this call, but their efforts ultimately came to little. The Black Death together with Tamarlane's conquests (he persecuted Christians and forced their conversion to Islam) marked the end of the second Christian penetration of China by the close of the fourteenth century.

Jesuit missionaries accompanied the sixteenth and seventeenth century Portuguese and Spanish explorers to China. At first, missionary activity was restricted to Macao, but after half a century of effort the Jesuits were finally permitted to enter China proper. The Jesuit strategy was to identify as fully as possible with Chinese custom and culture. The leader of this movement, Matteo Ricci, employed the Confucian heritage in particular as a bridge to the gospel, emphasising traditional belief in a high God or Lord of Heaven.[119] The Jesuits, in their 'adaptation' policy, were careful not to disrupt ancestor worship and its accompanying rituals. Thus arose the so-called 'rites controversy' which dragged on for over a hundred years. Ultimately, the Pope ruled against tolerating ancestral rites and in 1773 the Society of Jesus was dissolved.

What is to be said concerning the Jesuit approach? Ricci put all his eggs, as it were, in the Confucian basket, arguing that the 'true' Chinese tradition was Confucian, and that it was opposed to Buddhism but compatible with Christianity. However, as we have seen, neither Buddhism nor Confucianism offer Christian equivalents. The Pope rightly saw the Jesuit danger—already displayed by the Nestorians—to sell the gospel birthright for a mess of traditional Chinese potage. Would it not have been better to consider all the classic 'Three Religions' of China, as well as folk beliefs, to represent legitimate and commendable human striving to discover the truth, but as equally falling short of that goal? Where Buddhism gained strength in China at Confucianism's expense, Ricci's apologetic correspondingly lost persuasive force. St. Augustine, in his fifth century *Commentary on Genesis* had warned Christians not to couple revelational truth with human opinion so that when the latter fell by the wayside the gospel would suffer also.

Protestant missionaries appeared very late on the Chinese scene, the first being Robert Morrison in Macao in 1807. Did the absence of Protestant missionary work during the Reformation period and the great period of Protestant Orthodoxy signify (as Roman Catholic critics have suggested more than once) that Protestantism was inferior spiritually—indifferent to the needs of the lost?

The great Protestant missionary scholar Gustav Warneck of Halle regarded the Reformation in general and Luther in particular as anything but missionary-minded, and Warneck's negative evaluation has had much influence on lesser writers. Wrote Warneck in the standard *New Schaff-Herzog Encyclopedia of Religious Knowledge* (based on the great Herzog and Hauck *Realencyklopaedie*):

> The comprehension of a continuous missionary duty of the Church was limited among the Reformers and their successors by a narrow minded dogmatism combined with a lack of historical sense. They knew of the great missions of the past, but according to their ideas the apostles had already gone forth to the whole world and they and their disciples had essentially accomplished the missionary task. Christianity, therefore, had already proved its universal vocation as a world religion.

Elsewhere, Warneck stated that in Luther one misses not only 'missionary activity' but also the very 'idea of missions', and he refers to the reformer as hardly 'a man of missions in our sense of the word'. To which, Luther scholar Werner Elert replied sarcastically in his *Structure of Lutheranism*:

> Poor Luther! Instead of founding a missionary society, accompanying Cortez to Mexico, or at least assuring for himself a professorship of missionary science, he devoted himself, of all things, to the reformation of the church! . . . How could Luther, who expounded the Psalms, the Prophets and Paul, have overlooked or doubted the universal purpose of the mission of Christ and of His Gospel?

Indeed, Luther's writings abound in such passages as the following:

> Christians should bring forth much fruit among all the heathen by means of the Word, should convert and save many by eating about themselves like a fire that burns amid dry wood or straw; thus the fire of the Holy Spirit should consume the heathen according to the flesh and make room everywhere for the Gospel and the kingdom of Christ.[120]

It should be remembered that Roman Catholicism solidified its theological base as early as the thirteenth century (Thomas Aquinas died in 1250), thereby creating a 'launching pad' from which its missionary 'rockets' could be launched during the Renaissance and the Age of Discovery. Protestantism did not achieve a parallel theological base until the end of the seventeenth century—and the first Protestants (the Germans) were not a maritime power benefitting from exploratory contacts with the foreign field. Once the Netherlands and more especially England entered the lists, the age of Protestant missionary activity was born. As Latourette has shown in his monumental *History of the Expansion of Christianity*, the result in the eighteenth and nineteenth centuries was the greatest flowering of Christian missions in the entire history of the faith.

But what did Protestant missions achieve in China during the nineteenth and twentieth centuries? During the three decades immediately following Robert Morrison's arrival in Macao,[121] Protestant missionaries were subjected to Chinese law and custom and had access to China proper only by way of Macao and the traders' area outside the city of Canton (today's Guangzhou). Then came the infamous first opium war (1840). Western gunboat diplomacy was employed to produce the 'unequal treaties' that forced the Chinese to open five major ports to foreign trade and residence. It was at this time that Hong Kong was ceded to the British Crown under the long lease that will expire in 1997. From the 1840s, the principle of 'extra-territoriality' prevailed, which removed foreigners from the constraints of Chinese law and placed them solely under the more favourable jurisdiction of their own foreign consulates. The second opium war humiliated the Chinese government even further, and from that point on foreigners were allowed to live in the interior of China and also to become property owners.

The consequences of these political activities were naturally devastating for missions, whether Catholic or Protestant. From the Chinese perspective, Christians were identified with Western imperialists. The Tientsin massacre of 1870 was only surpassed by the Boxer rebellion in 1900—when 333 missionaries and children and thousands of Chinese converts were slaughtered. But even that appalling occasion was an opportunity to preach Christ; here is a first-hand account of the conversion of a Boxer executioner, who was told that no Boxer leaders would be punished, though they could not return to their villages unless they became Christians for fear that otherwise the atrocities would be repeated:

> Trusting to my word, a *chi-hsiung*, or executioner-in-chief, came back to the village. I shall never forget it, all my life. It was evening. I had just finished prayer and expounding the catechism, and I was peacefully smoking my pipe with my Christians, when a Christian broke in, followed by a stranger. When they saw him, I noticed the Christians shudder with horror. The stranger prostrated himself at my feet, trembling, and then got up, turned towards the assembled people and said, in a strangled voice, 'Christians, forgive me. I have done wrong' . . .
>
> One of the Christians stepped out of the crowd and said: 'You've got nothing to be afraid of Our law is a law of love, and we must love our enemies. If you want to become a Christian, there is no more anything between us: you will be our brother.'
>
> It was one of those scenes so striking that you think you must be dreaming . . . A few steps away some Christians, hiding so as to listen, and trembling more violently than the flame of the candle which made all these shadows shudder. And in the

> middle, prostrated with his head on the ground, the one who has sowed bereavement in every family, guilty a hundred times of death—and no one touched him or cursed him.[122]

Virulent Chinese opposition to the missionary movement was not only physical; it was also ideological, particularly in the decade of the 1860s. In 1861 there appeared the anonymous work *Pi-hsien chi-shih*, which was translated into English from an abridged version under the title. *Death Blow to Corrupt Doctrines*. This work 'for decades ranked supreme in the animals of Chinese anti-Christian literature',[123] and it became, the source of innumerable other books, tracts, and placards vilifying Christian faith. The *Death Blow* attempts to refute the arguments of such distinguished missionaries to China in that period as Griffith John.[124] But the impact of the work on its audience derives from the large amount of inventive libel it contains; it can well be considered the religious equivalent for that period of today's tabloid newpapers. Here are two typically juicy illustrations:

> Tso Tsung-te, a disciple of the barbarian rebel, Griffith John, arrived in Kiangnan and bought ten or so young girls from people who were in distressed circumstances. He placed them in a large residence. Each night, shortly after midnight, Tso, accompanied by two others, lit a lantern and stood in the middle reciting charms while all the young girls took positions around them. Presently blue smoke would emanate from the mouths of Tso and the others, the lantern light would suddenly brighten, and all of the young girls' clothing would fall off [mysteriously]. Tso and his associates, while standing, would then copulate with each of them in turn and blow on the girls' genitals. Hand in hand they would

then dance around in circles several times and all go to sleep. In time the owner of the house got wind of these goings on and promptly drove them out.

In Lichow [Hunan], recently, there was a rebel who had the power to make himself invisible and who, by means of black magic, cut off the queues of men, the nipples of women, and the testicles of little boys . . . Were you to ask [the victims] about this, they would in some cases say, 'I saw a priest wearing a cross on his chest. When he struck me I fell to the ground and, immediately becoming dizzy, could not stop him from doing what he did.' All the women and little boys who were thus injured suffered terribly upon reviving, and often died before a day had passed.[125]

Against the background of such calumny and danger, missionary activity in China in the second half of the nineteenth century entailed great heroism. The most striking examples are certainly Hudson Taylor and the founding of the China Inland Mission, the 'Cambridge Seven', and the work of the Student Volunteer Movement.[126]

James Hudson Taylor[127] was born in 1832 of Methodist parents near Leeds in Yorkshire, England. His father was a preacher. He had a powerful conversion experience at the age of fifteen, and both he and his father thought in terms of the dedication of his life to China. One of the influences on the young man was an appeal for Chinese missions written by a co-labourer of Robert Morrison. Hudson Taylor had begun medical studies but, having determined that his missionary focus should be in the area of evangelism, gave them up and sailed for China in 1853. He initially spent six years in gospel work there, married the daughter of a colleague with the London Missionary Society (two of Hudson Taylor's sons, a grandson, great-grandson and great-great-grandson would subsequently give their lives to China missions!), and came to rely for material support solely upon prayer—a principle that would become a defining mark of the China Inland Mission.

The next five years were spent in England for reasons of health, and during that time Hudson Taylor completed his medical course and formed the China Inland Mission. By 1911, it had grown to 968 missionaries and had contributions of $7 million without any campaigns to obtain funds. In 1866, Hudson Taylor returned to China. An American support base was created in 1888, due in part to Hudson Taylor's contacts with evangelist Dwight Moody at the Northfield Convention. Hudson Taylor retired to Switzerland in 1900, and in 1905 made his last journey to China, where he was received as a genuine patriarch. There he passed away and was buried with his first wife and those of his children who had died in China.

Hudson Taylor's theology was thoroughly biblical. He held to the verbal and plenary inspiration of the Scriptures and to their inerrancy. His heart went out to those who did not know Christ; on his way to China he wrote:

> Oh, what work for the missionary! Island after island, many almost unknown, some densely peopled, but no light, no Jesus, no hope full of bliss! My heart yearns over them. Can it be that Christian men and women still stay comfortably at home and leave these souls to perish? Can it be that faith no longer has power to constrain to sacrifice for His sake who gave His life for the world's redemption?

His philosophy of missionary work entailed total commitment to the proclamation of Christ's word:

> There is a needs-be for us to give ourselves for the life of the world, as He gave His flesh for the feeding

of the lifeless and of living souls whose life can only be nourished by the same life-giving Bread. An easy-going, non-self-denying life will never be one of power.

Fruit-bearing involves cross-bearing. 'Except a corn of wheat fall into the ground and lie, it abideth alone.' We know how the Lord Jesus became fruitful, not by bearing His Cross merely, but by dying on it. Do we know much of fellowship with Him in this? There are not two Christs—an easy-going one for easy-going Christians, and a suffering, toiling one for exceptional believers. There is only one Christ. Are you willing to abide in Him and thus to bear much fruit?[128]

The China Inland Mission drew the cream of England's evangelical, youth to China as the nineteenth century came to a close. The most dramatic example is certainly that of the so-called 'Cambridge Seven', who combined the ideals of Victorian 'muscular Christianity' with serious evangelical commitment. These men also contributed significantly to the work of the Student Volunteer Movement for foreign missions (the SVM).

Though himself a man of little education. Moody had conducted successful revivals at Yale and Princeton and had made a remarkable impression on British university youth during his two tours of Great Britain. Two Cambridge University athletes converted in his campaign of 1883, Charles T. Studd and Stanley P. Smith, made a stir in student circles on both sides of the Atlantic when with five others they volunteered for service in the China Inland Mission. Shortly before their departure for China, these men, dubbed the Cambridge Seven, toured

British universities on behalf of foreign missions, which set a precedent for the many SVM deputations to American colleges in later years. Studd's brother, J. E. K. Studd, who had been captain of the Cambridge cricket team and chairman of Moody's evangelistic meetings there, came to Northfield in the summer of 1885 at the urging of Moody and later that year began a speaking tour of American colleges and universities, which helped prepare the ground for the student movement about to come to birth in the United States.[129]

Of the Cambridge Seven, Dr. Eugene Stock wrote in the *History of the Church Missionary Society*.

The influence of such a band of men going to China as missionaries was irresistible. No such event had occurred before; and no event of the century has done so much to arouse the minds of Christian men to the tremendous claims of the Field, and the nobility of the missionary vocation. The gift of such a band to the China Inland Mission—truly it was a gift from God—was a just reward to Mr. Hudson Taylor and his colleagues for the genuine unselfishness with which they had always pleaded the cause of China and the world, and not of their own particular organisation, and for the deep spirituality which had always marked their meetings. And that spirituality marked most emphatically the densely-crowded meetings in different places at which these seven men said farewell. They told, modestly and yet fearlessly, of the Lord's goodness to them, and of the joy of serving Him; and they appealed to young men, not for their Mission, but for their Divine Master. No such missionary meetings had ever been

known as the farewell gathering at Exeter Hall on
February 4, 1885.

Remarkably, thirty years later six of the Cambridge Seven were still on the mission field, and the seventh would also have been there 'did circumstances permit'.[130]

What was the theology of the China Inland Mission (still going strong today as the Overseas Missionary Fellowship)?[131] It followed the biblical, evangelistic, pietistic style of its founder, and was more or less indifferent to confessional differences and theological profundities. CIM missionaries

> earnestly and always sought to convert individuals, deferring the development of churches. Accordingly, the mission was relatively indifferent to the type of church that was growing in a particular area, leaving it to the missionaries of the Anglican tradition here, or the Baptist tradition there, so long as there was reasonable continuity and freedom from confusion. Up to 1950 it was hard to discover just what was meant by "Nei ti hui" (Inland Mission churches). Missionaries of the China Inland Mission believed that it was right to leave their converts to God's guidance, without attempting to fit them to a church pattern.[132]

The same general approach was characteristic of the Student Volunteer Movement, whose motto was 'to win the world for Christ in this generation', and which made China a special focus of its attention. The SVM was the missionary arm of the intercollegiate YMCA and YWCA, which, prior to World War I, were still conservative and evangelical (it will be remembered that the great evangelical devotional writer Oswald Chambers—author of the classic, *My Utmost for*

His Highest—carried out most of his ministry under YMCA auspices). But the Student Volunteer Movement, like the China Inland Mission, was not interested in the niceties of systematic theology or ecclesiology.

> The SVM required no theological tests whatever but emphasised a warm, vital, practical piety and refused to become involved in doctrinal controversies. For the most part it avoided the liberal-conservative cleavage that was beginning to appear in American Protestantism. Faithful to the prevailing evangelical stance and temper, the SVM based its missionary appeal on the solid conviction of the universality of human sin and the resulting need of all mankind for salvation through Jesus Christ. Thus, the primary task of the missionary was assumed to be evangelistic, that is, to preach the gospel of Christ and serve as a personal witness to its saving efficacy. Yet from the outset evangelism was never conceived in narrow terms, and the claims of auxiliary undertakings, particularly medicine and education, were consistently placed before would-be volunteers no less urgency than was preaching.[133]

In 1911, the feeble Manchu dynasty collapsed in the face of reforming efforts and the Republic of China came into existence. During our time in China we visited at Nanjing the impressive mausoleum of China's first president, Dr. Sun Yat-sen—not incidently, a Christian. The other great leader during the Republic was Generalissimo Chiang Kai-shek of World War II fame; in Nanjing we stayed at a hotel which had once served as his military headquarters. Chiang Kai-shek and his wife were also believing Christians, but they were unable to cope with the fragmentation of central government authority brought about by rapacious local warlords who gained power in the vacuum left by the disappearance of the empire. The condition of the peasants and the common folk steadily worsened, opening the floodgates to Mao Tse-tung and the Communist takeover in 1949.

The period of the Republic was a very difficult one for Christian missions. Chiang Kai-shek's central government was supportive, but that government was weak, and local authorities—to say nothing of the warlords—were often highly resistant to what they regarded as foreign influence. The Second World War and Japanese aggression added greatly to the forces of destabilisation. Yet the missionaries continued and indeed expanded their influence. A well-known example—again in the tradition of Victorian 'muscular Christianity'—was Eric Liddell, subject of the internationally acclaimed, Academy Award-winning film, *Chariots of Fire*.

Liddell[134] was a Scottish evangelical athlete who refused to run on Sunday in the 1924 Olympic Games in Paris, but went on to win a gold medal and to set the world record in the 400 metre dash. A year later he left for China to devote the rest of his life to Chinese missions. Like his father, he served with the London Missionary' Society. For a time he taught science at the Anglo-Chinese college in Tientsin, and then engaged in rural evangelism—most of it using the standard Chinese means of locomotion, the bicycle. At the onset of World War II, Liddell sent his wife and two children to Canada for safety; his third child was born there. He was never to see the baby or his family again. Interned by the Japanese in 1943, he died at the age of forty-three in the internment camp just before the War ended in 1945. In the words of the closing credits of *Chariots of Fire*:

> Eric Liddell, missionary,
> died in occupied China
> at the end of World War II.
> All of Scotland mourned.

A child of missionary parents who was interned in the same camp wrote years later of his contact with Liddell there; the passage gives much insight into the character of the man.

> Sent to this same camp in Weihsien in August 1943 with many other missionaries' children, I will forever share with all the other hero-worshippers of my age that vivid memory of the man whom other prisoners described excitedly as the Olympic gold medalist who wouldn't run on a Sunday.
>
> Eric Liddell stood out among the 1800 people packed into our camp, which measured only 150 by 200 yards. He was in charge of the building where we younger children, who had already been away from our parents for four years because of the war, lived with our teachers. He lived in the very crowded men's dormitory near us (each man had a space of only three by six feet) and supervised our daily roll-call when the guards came to count us. One day a week 'Uncle Eric' would look after us, giving our teachers (all missionaries of the China Inland Mission and all women) a break. His gentle face and warm smile, even as he taught us games with the limited equipment available, showed us how much he loved children and how much he missed his own.
>
> Eric Liddell helped organise athletic meets. Despite the weakening physical conditions of the people as the war dragged on, the spirit of competition and camaraderie in sports was very good for us. Young and old watched excitedly, basking in the aura of Olympic glory as Eric Liddell ran in the race for veterans, his head thrown back in his characteristic style, sailing through to victory.[135]

What evaluation should be placed on the labours of the Protestant missionaries to China? On the positive side, the greatest of the historians of the Chinese missionary effort declares;

> Whatever may be one's opinion of the doctrines they taught, even a casual reading of their biographies cannot but bring the conviction that those who laid the foundation of future Protestant Churches did so usually with heroism and often at the sacrifice of comfort, health and even life. If to a later age, some of the beliefs of the pioneers seem antiquated and narrow, against these should be set the difficulties of learning a new language, the adjustment to unfamiliar . . . living conditions, the long struggle with ill health, the inconvenience of travel in an alien land, and the frequent unfriendliness and hostility of the populace and officials.[136]

At the same time, the actual results of a century of labour left much to be desired. The statistics very largely speak for themselves.[137]

	Chinese Communicants	*Missionaries*
1853	351	
1876	13.035	473
1903	122,800	2,785
1924	402,539	7,663
1949	823,506	6,204

When one remembers that China is the most populous country on earth, with population in 1949 of 540,000,000 (today it stands at 1,032,000,000!), it is difficult to avoid the conclusion that the Protestant churches lost an unparalleled opportunity to evangelise China. The number of missionaries was pitifully small in comparison with the need. The personnel problem becomes especially clear when one learns that 50 to 60 per cent of the missionaries were women: women missionaries laboured under tremendous disadvantages in a land where their activities were much limited and male volunteers simply did not appear. For all the talk about 'fulfilling the Great Commission', Western evangelical churches preferred their own comforts to the challenge of China. And into the spiritual vacuum created by a largely unevangelised China came the Marxist revolution of 1949.

Dr. Alan F. Gates, former missionary to Taiwan, poses the inevitable question:

> It remains only to ask the why of the apparent missionary failure and Communist success. The Communist movement shared most of the weaknesses which were found in Protestant missions. For example, they relied heavily upon a foreign benefactor—Russia, for prestige and power. Thus, in the early stages at least they patterned themselves after a European, not a Chinese, system of political thought. Quite often the Chinese Communists deliberately ignored and at other times openly attacked traditional Confucian values, seeking to eliminate the 'four olds' (habits, customs, thoughts and culture). Finally, the Communist movement has suffered continually from disunity within its ranks.

Why, then, did they succeed? Arthur Glasser suggests the reasons. First, there was a singleness of goal despite disunity in the party.

> Mao Tse-tung kept before his followers only one goal—political revolution. He was

> determined to bring about the complete transformation of Chinese society. This goal possessed him with the dynamism of a religious faith.

Second, the Communists were indigenous in character despite their leaning towards Russia in the early days.

> Mao Tse-tung . . . reinterpreted Marxism with reference to the Chinese experience and in the Chinese idiom. His revolutionary movement was Chinese in its leadership, recruitment, training of cadres and propaganda. Although Western in philosophy, he gave the Western profile . . . low visibility. The Chinese Communist Party had its own saints and martyrs, its charismatic leaders, songs and dramatic productions, its dances and slogans. It was a people's movement through and through.

The Chinese Church under Marxism and the Three-Self Movement

Under Mao Tse-tung a systematic effort was made to eliminate Christian influence in China. By 1952, virtually all missionaries had been forced out of the country. A systematic programme was developed to control and eventually immobilise Christian activity.[138] The first phase was to sever international Christian contacts: the church was to oppose imperialistic, foreign influences and to become thoroughly Chinese. Thus, a 'Chinese Catholic Church' was formed without any allegiance to the papacy at Rome, and all connections between Chinese Protestants and foreign Protestant denominations and ecumenical organisations were severed. Church leaders were persuaded that such changes were for the good of the church itself—a purification that would make the church less reactionary and more genuinely spiritual.

The second phase involved a full-scale subordination of the isolated Chinese church (only one recognised Catholic and one recognised Protestant church were allowed) to the state and its Marxist leadership and policies. Here the rallying cry was 'patriotism': the church must become truly patriotic in all its activity.[139] The decade of the 'cultural revolution' with the Gang of Four whipping youthful and ignorant Red Guards into active persecution of Christians (1966–1976) brought about the closure of churches throughout the land. A wall poster from this dark time well displayed the government's aims: 'We are atheists; we believe only in Mao Tsetung. We call on people to burn Bibles, destroy images, and dispense with religious associations.'[140]

And what was the result? The obliteration of Christianity in China? Exactly the opposite! The Chinese church went underground and experienced the most tremendous growth in its entire history! In 1949, when Mao came to power, the Christian population of China stood at some 823,000 souls, as we have seen. By 1982, the number had more than tripled to a total of 3,000,000. At the end of 1987, the Christian population had reached 4,000,000.[141] And today—forty years after the Maoist takeover and without the benefit of foreign missionaries—there are more than 5,000,000 members of official China Christian Council churches—to say nothing of thousands more in unofficial 'house churches'.

> The Beijing Christian Church has grown from 1,000 to 1,500 in two years. The Community Church in Shanghai has two Sunday services with an average attendance of, 1,500 at each service. Much of the growth is among young people and

students. These fellow believers are served by about 900 pastors, most of whom are quite old. There are 700 seminary students in thirteen seminaries, the largest in Nanjing with 200 students; a flourishing harvest field.[142]

What accounts for such amazing growth? Certainly the very fact of persecution has been a positive factor: the blood of the martyrs is the seed of the church. Church leaders in East Germany have ruefully noted an identifiable decline in churchgoing and church interest after the collapse of the Iron Curtain and the elimination of the church's persecuted status. But persecution in itself is not a sufficient explanation of church growth: sometimes (as with Pope Innocent III's medieval crusade against the Albigensians) the blood of the martyrs is simply the blood of the martyrs!

The most important single factor in explaining the explosion of the Chinese church during the Maoist period is surely its indigenisation: the fact that its survival came to depend solely on the Chinese believers themselves. This brings us incidentally to a look at the controversial Three-Self Patriotic Movement, which was formed in 1951 to rid the Chinese church of foreign dependency and to make it (1) self-propagating, (2) self-governing, and (3) self-supporting. This government inspired Movement (with its parallel Three-Self organisations for other religious groups such as Taoists, Buddhists, and Muslims) has received blistering criticisims for politicising the church and moving it in the direction of state control.

These criticisms have much legitimacy, especially during the early years of the Movement. In 1955, for example, one of the leading Chinese evangelical pastors who refused to co-operate with Three-Self was arrested, together with his wife and eighteen leaders of his church; here is the text of a letter that reached the West from Beijing concerning them:

Within the nation the spiritual warfare against the evangelical elements of the Church have risen to an unprecedented intensity against the faithful servant of the Lord Jesus, Mr. Wang Ming Tao, and his wife, and also his helpers and his deacons. Eighteen young Christians of college and university age, who, according to my knowledge, had participated in communion in Wang Ming Tao's place have been arrested by the government up to yesterday, charged with resistance to the Revolution. Praise God that they love their Lord, they are pleasing in His sight. God has permitted this thing to come to pass.

If one with spiritual insight would understand this thing, please read Luke 23:2. Today it is definitely evident that there are false prophets and false Christians. Under the banner of sins against the government, they have come forth to accuse Mr. Wang Ming Tao. Because they hate Jesus, they naturally hate His servant and those who love Jesus.

Mr. Wang Ming Tao was arrested about one o'clock in the morning of 8th August. On 7th August, Mr. Wang Ming Tao had given his last message. It was entitled, 'They in this manner betrayed Jesus.' The Spirit of Jesus made him understand the things that were coming to pass. His spirit would be faithful unto Jesus, even unto death. Mr. Wang Ming Tao gave out his last little booklet, 'We, Because of Our Faith.' . . . Peking has other servants of the Lord and believers who are already prepared to meet persecution. One can believe that in other places throughout the nation there will be true and faithful followers of the Lord who will be preparing to receive this grace.[143]

Pastor Wang was subsequently brainwashed into a 'confession', but after being released from prison renounced it; he was then reincarcerated.

But in recent years there is little doubt that the pendulum has swung in a different direction. Either the Three-Self Movement has become more genuinely Christian or Christians have been able to use it more effectively to further their own, rather than the state's purposes. Certainly the ideals of the Movement (self-support, self-governance, and self-propagation) represent the best objectives of indigenisation as taught by respectable missiologists. Three-Self was in large part responsible for the reopening of five thousand 'big churches' and some seventeen thousand registered meeting places after the fall of the Gang of Four. 'In many—although not all—cases, the government has restored church and seminary buildings to local Three-Self leaders and has paid back rent on buildings seized during the Cultural Revolution.'[144]

The charge has been made that the Three-Self Movement and the official Protestant Church have compromised fundamental Christian doctrine. Personal contact with the Nanjing Theological Seminary revealed an institution having considerable evangelical dynamism and a strong sense of continuity with the history of the church universal (note the student painting of Luther on the wall of the Christian Art class). True, the seminary does not rigorously exclude the use of higher critical methodologies in biblical interpretation, and one is troubled by articles in the official *Chinese Theological Review* such as 'Inspirations from Liberation Theology, Process Theology and Teilhard de Chardin.'[145] But it could be argued that willingness to flirt with such unfortunate Western theological deviations is actually a departure from the ideal of indigenous self-propagation!

In 1982, the China Christian Council published *Yao Dao Wen Da: 100 Questions and Answers on the Christian Faith*, a basic catechism which has been distributed in over seven hundred thousand copies; a corrected, second edition was issued in May 1987. This catechism provides an excellent means of evaluating the theology of the official Protestant church in China today. The worst that can be said of the catechism is that it lacks precision; thus, in its formulations on biblical authority, one looks in vain for descriptors such as 'infallible' or 'inerrant'. But there is no hint that the Bible should be taken other than as the final authority in all it says, and Trinitarian faith is proclaimed in accord with the Apostles and Nicene Creeds (which are specifically referred to as worthy of respect). Salvation is by grace through faith in Christ, and Eph 2:8 is cited in support of that paramount article of faith. The receiving of the Lord's Supper requires that one 'discern that it is the Lord's Body, not an ordinary meal' to avoid 'eating and drinking judgement on yourself'. As for Baptism, the Chinese church approaches it as does the Evangelical Free Church in the United States: 'Different local churches use either "sprinkling" or "immersion", depending on their own tradition or the request of the candidate.' Two questions in the catechism are particularly enlightening as to the theological orientation of Three-Self today:

58. In the period before Liberation, why was Christianity in our country regarded as a 'foreign religion'?

In the period before Liberation, there were some foreign Christians who loved the Lord, and who expressed their love by bringing the Gospel to our land. This was a good thing. But missionary work in those days was used by colonial and imperialist powers. They made the Chinese Church into an organisation belonging to foreign Churches, so that they depended for protection on unequal treaties which were imposed on China by foreign aggressors. All this was contrary to the teaching of the Bible, and gave the Gospel of Christ the ignominious reputation of being a 'foreign religion'. Moreover, it made it difficult for the Gospel to gain acceptance and become widespread among the mass of our people. For the policy in all religious activity should be: rely, not on might, nor on power, but on the Spirit of the Lord. Then only can it succeed (*cf.* Zech 4, Zech 6).

59. What gave rise to the suggestion of the Three-Self policy of the Chinese Church? What are the benefits of the 'Three-Self' movement?

A long time ago, before Liberation, some of our fellow-Christians advocated, on the basis of the biblical revelation, that the Chinese Church should be independent and self-governing. But in the situation prevailing at that time their ideas and efforts could not actually be put into effect. After Liberation, some of the leaders and ordinary Christians in the Chinese Church proposed, with a view to making a fresh start, carrying out self-government, self-support and self-propagation (abbreviated as 'Three-Self'). This proposal met with a ready response from the mass of Christians, and with the sympathetic support of all the Chinese people. The events of the past thirty years or so have clearly demonstrated that the Chinese Church, by supporting the Three-Self principles, has taken on a fresh appearance. Moreover, the relations between believers and those of our fellow-countrymen who have no religious belief are constantly improving. Carrying out the Three-Self principles has clearly been of great benefit to the Church, in expressing the truth of the Gospel, in asserting our national independence, and in ensuring the stability of the social order. It has clearly embodied the teaching of the Bible with regard to glorifying God and benefiting mankind (*cf.* 1 Cor 9:20, 1 Cor 9:21; Matt 5:16).

One of the most important analyses of Three-Self and its relationship to the direction of today's Chinese church was made by K. H. Ting, Vice-President of Nanjing University and President of the China Christian Council, in his 1984 Neesima Lectures at Doshisha University, Japan. It deserves to be quoted in extenso:

> You have noticed that the full name of the Three-Self Movement has the word 'patriotic' in it. Because of what has transpired under the word 'patriotism', there is a legitimate fear as to whether Three-Self is not a nationalistic or anti-foreign movement. This fear, however, is not warranted because Three-Self only aspires to make the church in China Chinese, that is, just as Chinese as the church in England is English and the church in U.S.A. is American.
>
> As to patriotism and nationalism we need to distinguish. There is the nationalism which gives its first loyalty to the nation or the state and upholds 'my country, right or wrong'. That is national chauvinism, under which criticism of wrong state policies is stifled and oppression and aggression justified. To call this patriotism is an abuse of the word which through the ages has acquired a content more noble and sublime. That Chinese Christians, especially their leaders, suffered so much during the cultural revolution for upholding their first loyalty to Jesus Christ and not to the political authorities testifies to the fact that when the word 'patriotism' is used by Chinese Christians, it is not used in that chauvinist sense.

On the other hand, there is the nationalism that is born of the people's effort to resist foreign encroachment in defence of national territory, national culture, and national language which are being trodden upon by a dominant power. This must not be equated with the nationalism of the aggressor. There are moments when small cultures, old cultures, cultures in which some great goodness and beauty reside, are being obliterated by the dominant force of a domestic autocracy or a transnational technological society, and when those who suffer from displacement and marginalisation rise up in self-defence to make life liveable. These occasions call Christians to choose to take the side of the people of their nation and be the supporters of a nationalism making for progress in history. Dr. Sun Yat-sen, a Christian, made a choice of this kind in his stand against Manchu despotism and foreign encroachment, and we are mindful of the support he got from friends in Japan . . .

The Chinese people suffered so much during the years of the Cultural Revolution and we Christians suffered so much with them. We have always felt that the gospel is something precious, but the Red Guards and the so-called rebels during the Cultural Revolution thought of it as nothing but a poisonous weed. We had no means of communicating it or of answering the attacks on Christianity in the big-character posters. Not a single church remained open in the whole of China. There was left no government organ to protect us from lawlessness. We were weak indeed, just a little flock. In all human reckoning, Christianity in China was for the fourth time in its history again breathing its last breath. But what we were blind to was that when we were weak and dying, life was in the offing. Strength is found in weakness, as life in dying. As Paul puts it, what you sow does not come to life unless it dies. What is sown is perishable, what is raised is imperishable. It is sown in dishonour, it is raised in glory. It is sown in weakness, it is raised in power. After having lost so much, we find there are more Christians in China than ever before, and more dedicated, too. After every church having been closed, we find that Christians are not only meeting in homes with great warmth, but that for five years now one church is being opened or reopened every day. Because we have been a part of the suffering fate of the Chinese people, we today are no longer so dissociated from them. We are in much better conversational relations with them than in the past. Thus, we seem to understand Paul when he said, 'We are afflicted in every way, but not crushed; perplexed, but not driven to despair; persecuted, but not forsaken; struck down, but not destroyed; always carrying in the body the death of Jesus so that the life of Jesus may also be manifested in our bodies,' (2 Cor 4:8–10) and all of this by the grace of God. The resurrection truth tells us that it is through loss, through poverty, through suffering and through death that life is sustained, in nation as well as in church. It tells us that life does not depend on power, or wealth, or property but on the risen Christ, the Lord of life who is also the ascended Christ sitting at the right hand of God and upholding the universe by His word of power. That a person who had died should come to life again is to all common sense an absurd claim. Yet almost one-fourth of humankind is committed to the resurrection story of Jesus. This is so because this message of hope has touched the chord of hope in the hearts of so many who simply refuse to accept defeat, humiliation, suffering, darkness, and death as ultimate, and who in the midst of all vicissitudes look up to the risen Christ. So, if I am to say in one or two words the most important and precious message that God has given to us in the last thirty-five years, I think one way to express it is the joy of the resurrection, the joy of knowing the risen Christ.[146]

What Western Christians Can Do for China

Indigenously the Chinese Church has made incredible advances in this generation. At the same time, the Tiananmen Square massacre displayed for the world to see that the government remains repressive, autocratic, and hostile to freedom of belief and opinion. On the one hand, efforts are made to soft-pedal traditional Marxist critiques of religion[147] on the other, persecution of Christian believers continues erratically.[148] Miller is correct that 'there is a checkerboard pattern of religious freedom across China because local government officers carry out national policies. Some have a relaxed attitude toward religion. But others . . . mistrust Christians and favour the older, hard-line policy of active suppression of religion'.[149] What can Western believers do to help their Chinese brethren and—in general—the citizens of that land where 3–4 June 1989 saw their worst fears come to life?

First and foremost, there is prayer. At the end of his life Hudson Taylor declared:

> I never was deeply interested in any object, I never prayed sincerely and earnestly for anything, but it came. At some time, no matter how distant a day, somehow, in some shape, probably the last I should have devised, it came. And yet I have always had so

> little faith. May God forgive me ... and cleanse the
> sin of unbelief from my heart.[150]

Since our Lord wishes 'all men to be saved and to come unto the knowledge of the truth' (1 Tim 2:4), praying for the salvation of the Chinese people is definitively prayer within the will of God. And our prayers need to be specific—for particular endeavours such as the congregations of believers mentioned in this book; the seminaries (that they maintain solidity of biblical doctrine and fervour of evangelistic spirit); Amity's printing of the Scriptures and Christian literature; and the leadership of the China Christian Council and the Three-Self Movement (that they continue to move from political conformity to scripturally-warranted furtherance of the indigenous church). Since even pagan rulers govern by God's sufferance to prevent anarchy (Rom 13), we are to pray for them—and this includes, to be sure, China's political leaders. Such prayers may even be of an imprecatory nature: I well remember my dear friend Dr. Harold Lindsell, editor emeritus of *Christianity Today*, telling me with satisfaction, after the premature death of Andropov, that he had prayed consistently for the demise of that former head of the KGB! And the students and others who took part in and continue to suffer for the ideals of the democracy movement of June, 1989, ought to have a special place in our prayers—that they not become isolated and discouraged; that they not weaken in the face of massive attempts to 're-educate' them; that they realise that ultimately what they stood for will prevail, for freedom cannot be repressed forever.

James H. Taylor III, great-grandson of Hudson Taylor and general director of Overseas Missionary Fellowship (formerly China Inland Mission), reinforces his great grandfather's words on prayer, and makes other valuable suggestions for Western Christians with a burden for China.

What then should our response be? If we were to ask Christians in mainland China what response they would value most highly, they would say 'We should value your prayers.' Join a prayer group and pray for mainland China. Thank God for greater religious freedom, for more open churches, for the house churches, for the older pastors as they faithfully preach and train new leaders.

The sponsoring of radio broadcasts for ministry to mainland China is probably the most effective way that we can actively support our brothers and sisters there.

Bibles have, as yet, been largely distributed in the major cities: there are thousands of Christians in the countryside who have none. Christian Communications Limited is involved in the preparation of a mini-library for pastors consisting of about twenty volumes, and apologetic literature is also now being prepared. There are opportunities for people to go into mainland China as English teachers, university teachers, doctors, accountants, agricultural consultants.

God is at work in mainland China today. 'I will build my church,' He said, 'and the gates of hell will not prevail against it.' There are five million Christians in mainland China, but more than 950 million still do not know Jesus Christ. Let us stand before the Lord faithfully for His work as it goes forward in mainland China today.[151]

Taylor speaks of the opportunities today to go to China in a secular capacity. The traditional role of missionary is no longer available in China, but one should remember that St. Paul insisted on maintaining a secular trade (tent-making, in his case), so as not to burden local Christians and their churches when he evangelised among them. Even after Tiananmen

Square, such opportunities have by no means disappeared; indeed, the regime is anxious to persuade Western business and industry to continue to expand in China, as we saw in chapter two. Thus the Western Christian still has wonderful opportunities to contribute directly to the spread of the gospel in China.

But a word or two of warning. First, the Westerner must lend his aid to the indigenous church—not endeavour to control it or lead it! The days of Western paternalism are long gone on the Chinese scene, and the Chinese—as the Three-Self Patriotic Movement well illustrates—are especially sensitive on the issue of foreign interference, even when motives are pure.

A second vital caveat relates to the theology of today's 'secular missionary'. Because he must obtain a secular vocation to enter China as a foreigner, and the time involved in training for it is often considerable (think, for example, of the physician or computer expert or engineer), the secular missionary often short-circuits full theological training, relying on little more than a Sunday School or Bible School knowledge of the faith. This is always a deadly mistake, and particularly so where China is concerned. We have seen that even the nineteenth-century missionary organisations such as the Student Volunteer Movement and the China Inland Mission were 'minimalists' theologically—putting questions of the sacraments, church polity, etc. aside while they concentrated on the evangelistic task. But the result was ultimately, under Maoism, a single Protestant church lacking in the kind of doctrinal precision and inerrantist view of Scripture so vital as bulwarks against the inroads of liberal theology. Even a great missionary hero such as Eric Liddell was very loose theologically: his pietistic sabbatarianism stood in tension with a pure grace view of justification and sanctification, and the religious writers he especially recommended (at the top of the list were Harry Emerson Fosdick and E. Stanley Jones!)

betray a frightening ignorance of the difference between a classic biblical orthodoxy and modern theological liberalism.[152] Today's secular missionary to China must do nothing to aid and abet the tendency in the Chinese church to emphasise the heart at the expense of the head. Indeed, he should arrive in China so thoroughly versed in the classic theology of Christendom that he can aid his Chinese brethren to much greater levels of theological depth.

James Taylor also mentions in passing the need for 'apologetic literature'. Such literature is vastly underrated in evangelical circles, but it is of tremendous importance wherever (and this means virtually anywhere today!) the gospel meets competition from other world-views. In China, the Christian is continually confronted by the viewpoints we discussed in chapters three and four: Marxism, traditional folk religion, Taoism, Confucianism, and Buddhism. What kind of apologetic approach is appropriate in these instances?

We pointed out a number of fundamental fallacies in each of these positions when we dealt with them, but it is essential to note that logically the refutation of one world-view never establishes the truth of another. To refute non-Christian positions hardly proves Christianity true.[153] One must offer positive and convincing evidence for the gospel, and to do that one must 'become a Jew to the Jew and a Greek to the Greek'—offering evidence that is persuasive in terms of the needs and mindset of the particular unbeliever.

It is legitimate to assume that today's Chinese is open to a search for truth. After all, did not the Third Plenary Session of the Eleventh Central Committee of the Chinese Communist Party announce in December 1978, after the fall of the Gang of Four, the new policy of 'emancipating the mind, using the brain, seeking truth from facts'?[154] Let us consider two prime common elements in the Chinese mindset as points of contact for apologetic evangelism. These elements derive from the exceedingly valuable study, *Ways of Thinking of Eastern Peoples*, published by the East-West Centre, Honolulu, and a product of the scholarly activity of Chinese and other Eastern scholars themselves.[155]

First, the Chinese display a 'conservatism expressed in the exaltation of antiquity', manifested in a 'continuity of the classical way of thinking' and the 'traditional character of scholarship'. Such traditionalism is particularly exhibited in the respect accorded to the written Chinese language; indeed, only the French among Westerners accord their language a parallel, almost religious veneration (among the French, it is said, grammatical faults are equivalent to moral faults!). Suppose, then, it could be shown that biblical truth is displayed in the inherent nature of the revered ancient Chinese script? This is precisely what has been argued by a Chinese pastor and scholar in a remarkable work of linguistic apologetics. Pastor Kang's co-author describes his discovery and gives representative Old Testament examples:

A VESSEL

舟

MOUTH
OR
PERSON

口

TO
CREATE

造

MOVE-
MENT
OR LIFE

Something that he had observed in a footnote of a Mandarin textbook used by a missionary came to mind. The character meaning *boat*, had been analysed as follows: a *vessel*; *eight*; and *mouth* or *person*. A comment followed that, interestingly, Noah's ark, the first great boat, had just eight passengers: Noah and his wife, with his three sons and their wives.

'If this is not mere happenstance, there should be other Biblically relevant characters,' reasoned Kang. Quickly he wrote down the character for *to create* and was astonished as he analysed the components in this figure for the first time: *dust* or *mud*; a *mouth; movement* or *life*; and *able to walk*. The text in Gen 2:7 came to his mind. 'Then the Lord God

BOAT

EIGHT

八

DUST
OR
MUD

土

WALKING

> formed man of *dust from the ground*, and breathed [with his *mouth*] into his nostrils the *breath of life*; and man walking became a living being' (not a baby but an adult, *able to walk*). Dissection of this character stimulated Pastor Kang's interest and resulted in a search which has lasted four decades.[156]

The same amazing correspondences apply also to the New Testament message:

> Now I wanted to focus on the New Testament Messiah, represented by such a multitude of symbols and types in the Old Testament. Why did He say to the woman at the well in Samaria, 'Whoever drinks of the water that I shall give him will never thirst; the water that I shall give him will become in him a *spring of water* welling up to *eternal life*' (John 4:14)? How incredible that the Chinese in the character for *eternal* obviously uses the *water* radical! A *point* • at the top of the figure signifies an 'anointing' or 'dedication' . . .

WATER 水

ETERNAL 永

TREE

> Now we move to Calvary. A cross—a *tree*—was created with Jesus nailed to it. This was the Man known by the multitudes for His miracles and teachings; envied by His brothers for His virtue; loved by His followers for His wise, kind, and gentle manner; hated by the priests for His authority, which was interpreted

as blasphemy when He said, 'Your sins are forgiven,' and for His claim to be the Son of God.

The very elements of nature could not endure seeing God's Son so cruelly treated. The day became mysteriously dark and ominous. When He breathed His last, He expressed it in the words: 'It is finished!' and He committed Himself into His Father's hands. Not believing He was already dead, a Roman soldier pierced His side, and there came out blood and water. THE SACRIFICE OF THE AGES WAS COMPLETE. The Seed of the Woman had been bruised. The unblemished Lamb of God had given His divine life for all—the Bread was broken, and there was more than enough for everyone. The *Water of Life had* gushed out 'for with Thee is the fountain of life' (Ps 36:9). *The Cross of Calvary had become the Tree of Life to all who would partake!*

TREE

木

ETERNAL

永

PATTERN OR EXAMPLE

樣

These three figures: the *tree*, the *lamb*, and *eternal* (*water*) are united into one glorious character meaning *example, pattern*! What more appropriate, complete, and meaningful symbolism could be used to portray our great Exemplar? It would seem that the ancient Chinese sage was truly inspired to draw together these completely symbolic figures and produce a totally meaningful character. He surely appears to have been thinking God's thoughts after Him![157]

LAMB

WATER

A second common feature of the Chinese mindset is, according to Nakamura and his associates, 'perception of the concrete', with 'emphasis on the particular'; this has meant a 'lack of consciousness of universals', the 'non-development of abstract thought' and general indifference to metaphysics. When taken in conjunction with the Chinese Marxist programme of 'seeking the truth from facts', this orientation should provide considerable openness to the particularised claim of the gospel that God came to earth historically in Jesus Christ for our salvation. Christianity, unlike the Western metaphysical tradition (think of Platonic and Hegelian idealism), does not move from the general to the specific; rather, it takes its point of departure from the concrete particularity of the Incarnation in historical time and geographical space. Understandably, therefore, the style of apologetics represented by my book *History, Law and Christianity*, which sets forth the overwhelming historical case for Jesus Christ, can be of immense value in presenting the gospel to today's inquiring Chinese thinker.

And when this particularised, concrete historical fact is driven home, it can displace the harmonising tendency of the Chinese to blend all beliefs into an uneasy synthesis. After all, the God who demonstrably came into history for our salvation declares in no uncertain terms that he is 'the way, the truth, and the life' and that there are no substitute religious routes to eternal bliss (John 14:6; *cf.* Acts 4:12). If the response is that such a conclusion entails logical reasoning, and the Chinese never developed a system of formal logic, we simply reply with Nakamura that 'if "rational" means thinking in a practical utilitarian way then it is the Chinese rather than the Westerners who are far more rationalistic'.[158] Rationally and practically, if God did indeed enter this world to save us, and he tells us that we need that salvation and no other, it would be the height of folly, individually and nationally, to ignore his message.

Is There Hope for China?

China has suffered across the centuries from an authoritarian—indeed totalitarian—tradition, and its current leadership has been living off that inherited capital. Can we then expect Deng's gerontocracy to reduplicate itself for the foreseeable future and the people passively to ingest 'unfreedom' as a staple diet?

Surely not—and for three reasons. First, in Tiananmen Square the regime made the fatal mistake of slaughtering students. If there is any Chinese tradition stronger than imperial subservience, it is that of respect for 'the scholar'.[159] The martyrdom of the students on 3-4 June 1989 will forever rise to haunt the Marxists guilty of it and provide a rallying point for future resistance.

Secondly, freedom once tasted can never be permanently eliminated. Ever since the end of the Gang of Four (1976), the regime has committed the grave error of encouraging communications from the outside world. Students have gone abroad and returned with personal experience of freedom. Westerners have been invited to lend their expertise to the modernisation of the Chinese economy. The lumbering dinosaur that constitutes any planned economy required the leadership to increase contact with healthy economies elsewhere. But these contacts inevitably brought the fresh winds of freedom with them. Now there is no way to turn the clock back, and the examples of the violent death of Communism throughout Eastern Europe and the revitalisation of the U.S.S.R. via *glasnost* and *perestroika* add fuel to a flame that will ultimately consume China's old guard.

Finally, we need to keep in mind the source of all true freedom. 'If the Son therefore shall make you free,' declared Jesus, 'ye shall be free indeed' (John 8:36). The original source of all 'unfreedom' is sin—the selfishness that treats others as objects instead of persons and uses power to debilitate others for our advantage. God is the author of all genuine liberty, for his act on the cross for us provides the only ultimate liberation from our self-centredness. He is always on the side of liberty, and those who strive for it can have the confidence that behind the corridors of history he works to maximise it. May China recognise the true source of the freedom it so desperately seeks and enter into a living relationship with the Tao made flesh.

PART TWO

ESSAYS FOR CONTEMPORARY CHRISTIAN SINOPHILES (AND FOR CYNICAL RELIGIOUS LIBERALS AND PAGANS)

WHY YOU SHOULD NOT BUY INTO CONFUCIANISM

*J*nterestingly enough, as liberal theologians reach the end of their careers, they often plunge into a study of Eastern religiosity. Examples: John Hick; D. Z. Phillips and Ninian Smart (some years ago, in 1993, Phillips, Smart, and I were featured speakers on the same university religion panel at the California State University at Fullerton)[160]; and—to be sure—Paul Tillich.[161]

The motivation for such interest surely stems in large part from the common belief among liberal religious thinkers that, if we penetrate deeply enough into their mindset, all religions are really saying the same thing, and salvation is available in those contexts, not just in Christianity. Ninian Smart: 'I often say that I'm a Buddhist-Episcopalian.'[162]

Now, *mirabile dictu*, I am myself swimming in the infinite ocean of Eastern religiosity, but (1) this is not something new, since the first edition of *Giant in Chains: China Yesterday and Today*, was published in German and in English decades ago,[163] and (2) I have become convinced that, the more carefully one studies the primary sources of the Eastern religions, the *less* they can be reconciled with historic Christianity—and the *less* they show compatibility with biblical teaching on salvation. If this is indeed the case, the implications could not be more serious, for Christianity is an exclusive faith, claiming unique truth-value.[164]

In this brief essay, we shall illustrate the gulf separating Confucianism and biblical religion by way of several Chinese word studies.

The Confucian Moral Landscape and Its Consequences

Confucius himself was little interested in the next world; his teachings focus on the proper ethic for personal and societal life in this world. He was a strong advocate of authoritarianism in the home and in the state: ancestors were to receive the highest respect, parents were to be revered by their children, and the masses were to accept the final authority of rulers.

Such a belief-system fits nicely into the totalitarian philosophy of today's People's Republic of China, with its thoroughgoing Marxist orientation. (I have argued already that there really was never a 'Last Emperor', for the imperial mindset continues in authoritarian Chinese Marxism.) This may be at least one explanation for the Party's lauding of Confucianism and its careful control of Christian religious organisations in the country, as well as the Party-led persecution of Christian believers who do not follow, or who have the temerity to criticise, state policies.

A study of key terms representing Confucian values offers a clear picture of what salvation has meant for centuries in the Chinese context. Particularly helpful in this regard—in spite of its limitations—is Barbara Aria's little book, *The Spirit of the Chinese Character*, and the quotations to follow can be located there under the particular characters discussed.[165]

道 **(dào)**. The concept of Tao was far more important to Taoism than to Confucianism. For Lao-tze, the 'Way' designated the universal Absolute, approachable through mystical negation: *wu-wei*, 'non-striving/deedlessness'. Confucius, who engaged in personal discussion with the founder of Taoism, found his path essentially incomprehensible. Confucius' was a more earthly, practical route. 'To Confucius *tao* became the "way" of moral rectitude—the way we do what we do.' It seems unarguable that Confucius regarded the Tao *humanistically*, not metaphysically, and this fits with the etymology of the term: the character combines the notions of 'head/chief/first' and 'movement' (pictograph of a foot)—suggesting forward progress and perhaps the following of a leader (a plumed authority figure). But progress directed where? and following what authority or leader?

Translators of the New Testament into Chinese have invariably (for wont of something better) employed *dào* to represent the 'word made flesh' of John's Gospel; but it is plain that no Chinese ideology uses the concept to declare that the transcendent personally enters history.

In accord with Confucius' stress on the values vital to a good society, early Confucian tradition focused on a number of ethical 'Constants'. Some of the most fundamental of these warrant our attention here.

仁 **(rén)**. This central Confucian virtue generally translates as 'benevolence'. 'Considered by Confucius as innate in humans, [it] can also be translated as "kindness" or "humanity." The ideas are inseparable. . . . This ideogram combines the radical for "human being" (also pronounced *jên* [*sic*]), showing the legs and trunk of a person, with the pair of horizontal strokes that denotes "two." Benevolence: the essential kindness that one person shows to another.'

But, to be sure, the 'innateness' of kindness and benevolence is denied by the overwhelming testimony of human history—and should have been evident to Confucius himself by observing the cruelty of Chinese authorities to those who opposed them and their continual efforts to capture and rule the lands of others (*cf.* the period of the Warring States that began just a few years before Confucius' death).

義 (**lì**).[166] This character, representing 'righteousness', displays a sheep above the sign for 'I/me/myself'. The idea is that one must act in the manner of a docile and selfless sheep. 'Confucianism insists on righteousness, one of the ... inborn virtues which, if cultivated, can purify our spiritual energy. ... Mencius defined [it] as doing what we should as "citizens of the universe," while Confucius stressed doing what we should purely for its own sake, without desire for material or spiritual gain.'

It would be interesting to know how many sheep-like people Confucius met, particularly among the Chinese aristocracy. In the Confucian context, one is at a loss to find the biblical notion of 'lost sheep'—and therefore there appears to be no need for a Good Shepherd who gives himself for the little lambs and the wandering sheep he loves.

安 (**ān**). 'Tranquillity/peace' is an important Confucian virtue. 'The character for "tranquility" is rooted in the ancient Chinese tradition of male dominance. A "woman" under a man's "roof" indicates that all is as it should be. But *an* has a richer meaning, reflecting the parallel between microcosm and macrocosm. Just as a harmonious relationship between man and woman brings tranquility to the heart, peace comes when universal energies are in harmony—the forceful, creative energy of heaven above, and the gentle, receptive energy of the earth below. Tranquility: when our world is in order.'

Fine. But *how* do we put the world, above or below, in order? Not just feminists would question the male/female dichotomy here. For the human microcosm to get right with the cosmic macrocosm, a bit of self-awareness of our egocentrism might be the appropriate starting-point. That, however, would require a serious look at sin and human depravity—not a subject in the Confucian philosophical/religious curriculum.

慈 (**cí**). Young, tender grass is pictured above the human heart, suggesting a softening of the spirit and the resulting presence of compassion, benevolence, kindness, and charity. 'It is natural for us to want to help those in need, especially the young and helpless. This is why many Confucians believed in the essential goodness of human nature. If we see a child fall into a well, for instance, we automatically try to save the child.'

Do we? In continental, French law, it is indeed a criminal offence if a capable person sees another in peril and does nothing to help. But in Anglo-American law (except where statute has replaced the common-law tradition), one is culpable only if one *commences* to render help and then *ceases* to assist.[167] In fact, kindness is hardly an inherent, universal human quality. Being nasty to your neighbour has been practised far more across the geographical and historical landscape than charitable benevolence.

忠 **(zhōng)**. Loyalty had a position of great importance in the Confucian hierarchy of values. The Hanzi character representing it displays at the top an arrow penetrating a target at its very centre; beneath is the human heart. 'This shows that loyalty—whether it is to country, person, or principle—means having a centered heart. A heart that is in the center is a heart in the right place.'

One can hardly argue against the virtue of loyalty as such. The problem is to determine *what* authority, institution, or person is *worthy of becoming the object of the loyalty*. There was unreflective loyalty to Adolf Hitler and his ideology by an entire generation of young Germans (the *Hitlerjugend* and its equivalents), and the results were appalling and damnable. But nowhere in Confucianism do we find the absolute moral criteria for deciding where our loyalties should be placed.

* * *

To be sure, not all Confucian masters followed Confucius himself and his most famous disciple, Mencius, in their belief in the inherent goodness of human nature. The most important of the Confucian 'revisionists' was certainly the third century B.C. author or authors of the *Xunzi*, a work of considerable intellectual strength, long neglected owing to the popularity of Mencius.[168] Chapter 23 is titled 'Human Nature Is Bad' and argues:

> People's nature is bad. Their goodness is a matter of deliberate effort. Now people's nature is such that they are born with a fondness for profit in them. If they follow along with this, then struggle and contention will arise, and yielding and deference will perish therein. They are born with feelings of hate and dislike in them. If they follow along with these, then cruelty and villainy will arise, and loyalty and trustworthiness will perish therein. They are born with desires of the eyes and ears, a fondness for beautiful sights and sounds. If they follow along with these, then lasciviousness and chaos will arise, and ritual[169] and *yi*, proper form and order, will perish therein. Thus, if people follow along with their inborn dispositions and obey their nature, they are sure to come to struggle and contention, turn to disrupting social divisions and order, and end up becoming violent. So, it is necessary to await the transforming influence of teachers and models and the guidance of ritual and *yi*, and only then will they come to yielding and deference, turn to proper form and order, and end up becoming controlled. Looking at it in this way, it is clear that people's nature is bad, and their goodness is a matter of deliberate effort.[170]

The *Xunzi*, though a vast improvement on the classical Confucian view of man's 'inherently good nature', is still not at all compatible with biblical Christianity. Note that, for the *Xunzi*, the evil nature of man is capable of correction by the example of good 'teachers and models'. The insoluble difficulty here is that if, as is surely the case, human beings are self-centred, where can one find the 'good teacher and model'? And, if found, how did that teacher or model acquire his/her goodness, since *all* 'human nature is bad'? In biblical Christianity, that problem is solved by the coming to earth of God's own Son—the Good Master, who could say, 'Which of you convinceth me of sin?' (John 8:46).

And if one's 'goodness is a matter of deliberate effort', then one can save oneself—in diametric opposition to the biblical teaching that salvation is a gift of God, the result of grace received by faith in the Saviour, 'not of works, lest any man should boast' (Eph 2:8-9).

Of course, in fairness to the *Xunzi*, its author or authors had no contact with the biblical *Heilsgeschichte*: the promise and ultimate appearance of the Messianic saviour. At least, though there is no realistic solution offered, the *Xunzi* shows far greater awareness of man's fundamental moral problem than can be found in Confucius or in Mencius.

Concluding Reflection

One of the cardinal rules in the study of comparative religions deals with the relationship between sin and salvation: *errors as to the nature or effects of sin will inevitably corrupt one's doctrine of redemption*. This is painfully evident in cults such as Christian Science and Scientology, where the absence of any serious view of the human sinful condition totally cancels out Christ's sacrificial death on the cross as the answer to and the remedy for the sins of the world.

The same is surely the case with Confucianism. Human nature is far from 'intrinsically good'. And the Confucian moral principles, as attractive as they appear linguistically, have no more force in a sinful world than the Boy Scout Oath and Law.[171]

There is, of course, an inherent, built-in morality within every human person. God's will in creation ensured that, and the fall of man did not destroy man's humanity (Rom 1). But that original knowledge of what is right and what is wrong has been so corrupted by man's sinfulness that it cannot be naïvely relied upon. A special revelation from God almighty is the sine qua non for distinguishing genuine morality and social values from sheer self-centredness. The Bible is the essential guide to what is 'natural law' and what is mere human egoism passing itself off as morality and ethics.

In sum, *don't go Confucian*. Go biblical! In Holy Scripture, you will receive all the moral benefits offered by Eastern wisdom—together with an infinitely more realistic view of human nature. Beyond this, you will find that salvation is indeed available, and to you personally—at an infinite cost to God but given to you as a free gift when you accept his Son as your Saviour. 'If any man be in Christ, he is a new creature: old things are passed away; behold, all things are become new' (2 Cor 5:17).

THE GOSPEL ACCOUNTS

Historical Fact or Narrative Fiction?

The New Testament is seen by more and more traditionally conservative evangelical scholars as the product of literary/dramatic construction, in line with stylistic characteristics found in classical (Greco-Roman) literature or ancient Jewish writing outside of the Bible. Examples of scholars employing this approach include evangelical Michael Licona and Lutheran James Voelz.

First, Licona:

> There is somewhat of a consensus . . . that the Gospels belong to the genre of Greco-Roman biography (*bios*). . . . Because *bios* was a flexible genre, it is often difficult to determine where history ends and legend begins.[172]

> I have noted above that that there is now somewhat of a consensus . . . that the Gospels belong to the genre of Greco-Roman biography (*bioi*) and that this genre offered biographers a great deal of flexibility to rearrange material [and] invent speeches to communicate the teachings . . . of the subject.[173]

[*Cf.* Lydia McGrew's comprehensive critique, *The Mirror or the Mask: Liberating the Gospels from Literary Devices* (Tampa, FL: DeWard, 2019).]

Second, Voelz:

> In excursus 3, 'Literary Assumptions regarding Mark's Gospel,' we introduced the notion that there are significant parallels between the contours of Mark's narrative and the story of the *Odyssey*, and we sought to demonstrate these parallels in relevant pericopes.[174]

[Even though Voelz does not expressly state that the alleged parallels in Homeric literature mean that Mark allowed fiction to colour Gospel fact, he does not disallow that possibility. If Mark was indeed saying (*mirabile dictu!*) that Jesus was greater than Odysseus, would it not be far better to conclude that the reason Jesus' history in fact surpassed Homer's story was that, in Jesus' case, the narrative represented *what actually occurred*?][175]

Is the literary methodology set forth by these New Testament scholars consistent with the evangelical and Reformation belief in the entire truth of the Holy Scriptures, as well as with the conviction underlying the Ecumenical Creeds of Christendom (Apostles', Nicene, and Athanasian) that the New Testament conveys a reliable historical portrait of the earthly life of our Lord?

We do not think so.

First, a logical point—to be followed by an analogy and, ultimately, a warning.

Aside from the serious failings in the employment of literary argument, as analysed in detail by Lydia McGrew, one must ask this question: Is it reasonable to begin with literary devices employed by writers other than an author, and conclude—against the author's own express statements (e.g., Luke 1; 2 Peter 1:16; 1 John 1:1)—that he must be using the same literary devices as some other writers employed during the same cultural era?

Whatever happened to the inductive principle that an author must be taken to be doing what he says he is doing, and that he has every right *not* to be using literary devices that his contemporaries choose to employ? Forcing an author into the Procrustean bed of what other writers are doing violates the logical principle that to understand something or someone, one must move from the specific to the general, not start with the general and force the specific to accord with it. One must respect an author's stated position, as found in what he says and how he presents his material—as Aristotle well argued in his *Poetics*.

And now, here is an analogy. Sir Walter Scott, in his nineteenth-century novel *Ivanhoe*, presents the classic literary image of the heroic knight. His novel exemplifies elements of the Romance genre: the quest with chivalric setting, the overthrow of a corrupt social order, and the achievement of a millennial time of joy.[176] This Romantic-hero motif has powerfully influenced Western literature to the present day (Tolkien, *et al.*).

Suppose, therefore, a hundred years from now a literary scholar argues that the story of Charles de Gaulle's leadership in freeing France from the Nazi occupation is a literary creation. After all, it has all the essential elements: a fairly low-level military officer reaches England[177] and is virtually ignored by the American and English leadership[178] but becomes the greatest hero of the French nation in the twentieth century. Indeed, almost every village in France today has an *Avenue Charles de Gaulle*.

So, even though the historians claim that their story of de Gaulle is factual history, the literary interpreter can argue that they must have been influenced, consciously or unconsciously, by the Romantic tradition in penning their accounts. Their affirmations of historical truth can be trumped by the application of sophisticated literary analysis.

If we rightly reject such an approach in general, we must surely reject it when applied to the New Testament records.

And to claim that the literary interpretive methodology is 'just a matter of hermeneutics', having no impact on the doctrine of biblical inspiration and authority, is patent nonsense. A generation ago, a seminal article was published with the title, 'Hermeneutics as a Cloak for the Denial of Scripture',[179] and the point of that article remains exactly the same today: any interpretive method that dehistoricises the Bible destroys its claim to truth and thus its divine authority.

In discussing 'the pragmatic status of narrative fiction', French specialist Jean-Marie Schaeffer notes, 'The conditions for satisfying the criteria of factual narrative are semantic: a factual narrative is either true or false. Even if it is willfully false (as is the case if it is a lie), what determines its truth or its untruth is not its (hidden) pragmatic intention, but that which is in fact the case.'[180] Gospel narratives, therefore, if they are essentially literary constructions and not representative of historical fact, can be neither true nor false—and are thus incapable of being regarded as constituting truth—much less infallible or inerrant divine revelation.

In terms of what we have argued here, it should not appear strange that we conclude with a most serious warning—especially as to how one evaluates contemporary New Testament scholarship. Do not believe that just because an evangelical or a Lutheran teaches at a distinguished institution that has historically stood for a strong view of Scripture that he or she necessarily holds to biblical factuality or to a meaningful view of scriptural inerrancy. Princeton Theological Seminary was allowed by its sponsoring church body to depart radically from the classical Reformed view of Holy Scripture because no one could believe that this might occur at the faculty of theology where B. B. Warfield had once taught.

Santayana's adage still applies: 'Those who cannot remember the past are condemned to repeat it.'

WHY NOT REGARD THE GOSPEL NARRATIVES AS FICTIONAL CONSTRUCTS?

*A*n influential number of evangelical and Lutheran biblical scholars are arguing that the gospel writings reflect either a Jewish *Midrash* or a Greco-Roman authorial style that presents as historical fact what is actually literary construction.[181]

How do we determine if, in fact, this is what occurs in the case of the New Testament narratives?

Let us move away from the emotionally charged material that is the subject of these allegations to an entirely different realm: that of the Chinese supernatural tale. Such tales are one of the very earliest examples of Chinese literary art.[182]

Consider 'The Fairy of Chinghsi Temple',[183] a narrative included in the fifth–sixth-century A.D. classic 齊諧續記 (More tales of Chi Hsieh).

THE FAIRY OF CHINGHSI TEMPLE

When Chao Wen-shao of Kuaichi was the crown prince's steward, he lived near Central Bridge at Chinghsi, about two hundred paces from Minister Wang Shu-ching's house in the next alley. One autumn night superb moonlight made him homesick, and leaning on his gate he sang that melancholy song 'Crows Fly in the Night'. Then a maid of about sixteen, dressed in blue, came up to him.

'Greetings from my young mistress in the Wang family,' she said. 'She heard you sing while we were playing in the moonlight, and sends her regards to you.'

As it was still early and not everyone had retired, Chao was not unduly surprised. He answered politely, and invited the young lady over.

In a short time she appeared. She seemed eighteen or nineteen, her gait and air were sweet, and she had two maids with her. Chao asked where she lived.

'Over there.' She pointed toward the minister's house. 'When I heard you sing, I decided to call. Will you sing something for me?'

Then Chao sang 'Grass Grows on the Rock'. He had a clear and melodious voice, and she enjoyed the words too.

'If you have a pitcher,' she said, 'you need not be afraid of lacking water.' She turned to her maids and told them: 'Go back and fetch my cithern, and I shall play to this gentleman.'

Presently the cithern was brought, and she played two or three haunting and plaintive airs. Then she bade her maids sing 'Heavy Frost' and loosening her belt to fasten the cithern to her waist played an accompaniment. The song went like this:

Dusk falls, a cold wind blows,
Dead leaves cling to the bough;
Alas, you cannot know
The love my heart holds now!
The curtains of my bed
Are white with heavy frost;

> The frost is falling still,
> And I alone am lost.
>
> After this song it was late and she spent the night with him: departing at the fourth watch just before dawn. She left him her gold hairpin as a keepsake. In return Chao gave her a silver bowl and white glass spoon.
> When day broke Chao went out and happened to pass the temple. Going in to rest by the shrine, he was surprised to find the bowl there, while behind the screen he discovered the glass spoon. The cithern still had a belt attached to it. In the temple stood the image of the fairy, with maids dressed in blue before her—the same whom he had seen the night before! This took place in the fifth year of Yuanchia (428). But Chao never had another adventure of the kind.

Note that the narrative of the miraculous appearance and activity of a supernatural being (the fairy) begins and ends with specific historical references: the minister is named, the geographical location is identified (the Central Bridge at Chinghsi), and the story is given detailed dating (the fifth year of Yuanchia [428]).

Can one then analogize to the gospel stories and argue successfully that they, too, are literary narratives placed in a historical context to give them more force? Could not the birth of our Lord 'in the days of Caesar Augustus' and the climax of his miraculous earthly career in a trial involving the Roman governor Pontius Pilate be seen as the historical embellishments of a literary tale?

The answer is an emphatic *no!*

Our Chinese tale is in a different category—not because it contains a supernatural element (since we live in a contingent, relativistic universe, we are in no position whatever metaphysically to rule out certain events as 'impossible' a priori)[184]—but for a variety of other reasons.

The following interpretive principles are fundamental. They should be followed when dealing with the gospel records, just as with narratives in general:

1. If an author sets forth his material as representing historical fact, as does Luke in the prefaces to his Gospel (1:1–4) and to the Acts of the Apostles (1:1–3), one must presume that that is the case. In stark contrast, the Chinese tale set forth here was penned by the littérateur Wu Chun (吳均; 469–520), a 'well-known poet with a distinctive style'.[185] His tales are understood to reflect a literary rather than an historical perspective.
2. If the story is reported by eyewitnesses or close associates of eyewitnesses within a reasonable time after the events described—as is the case with the gospel accounts[186]—there is good reason to consider the story factually true. Our Chinese supernatural story is not reported by an eyewitness; it is said to have occurred before the author was born and is reported by him some eighty years after the events in the tale were supposed to have occurred.
3. If the historical claims of a document are limited to its introduction and conclusion (as with our Chinese tale), suspicions can legitimately be raised. In the New Testament records, the historical references are not so limited to the beginning and the ending of Jesus' earthly ministry but are present *throughout* (John the Baptist's death at the hands of King Herod, details concerning the Pharisees and Sadducees, etc., etc.).

4. Collateral historical data, nowhere available in the case of the Chinese story but powerfully compelling for the gospel records, will support the historicity of the latter. *Cf.*, as just one example, the onomastic correlation statistics of personal names in the gospels that cannot be found outside the narrow time frame of Jesus' Palestine.[187]
5. If a story is offered by a single writer, it will have far less historical force than if several writers (even if they collaborate) provide similar narratives. The four gospels are a strong historical support for the historicity of the data in any one of them.

In conclusion, those who would in any way engage in historical reductionism where the New Testament documents are concerned would do well to spend time with comparative literature. In that way, the immense differences between gospel historicity and creative literature might eventually penetrate their hermeneutic vagaries.

WHY TWO EXCELLENT NINETEENTH-CENTURY SCHOLARS REJECTED BIBLICAL TRUTH

*F*or the serious Christian believer, hardly anything is more painful than learning of the departure of the learned from biblical Christianity. 'Why does this occur?' we invariably ask ourselves. Some answers to this question can be found in two widely separated nineteenth-century instances—one focusing on England and China, the other on Germany and the Lutheran Church–Missouri Synod in the United States of America.

Herbert Allen Giles

Few sinologists are remembered beyond their own time, and then only by a narrow circle of specialists in their field. But Herbert Giles, professor of Chinese at Cambridge University, is a remarkable exception. With his predecessor, Thomas Francis Wade, the first professor of Chinese at Cambridge, he created a vitally important romanisation system for the Chinese language (known as the Wade-Giles system), providing an alphabetic representation of Chinese characters and thereby facilitating the learning and reading of Chinese beyond anything possible earlier.[188] Among Giles' many publications is the most extensive translation of Pu Songling's seventeenth/eighteenth-century classic, 聊齋志異 (*Strange*

Stories from a Chinese Studio), a rendering of high literary quality accompanied by valuable historical and cultural notes.[189]

Giles' translation has, however, been criticised as 'prudish'[190] for his bowdlerising of a number of the Chinese stories by omissions or by 'cleaning up' the text to remove material that would offend Western readers because of sexual or repugnant content. Such moralism might suggest that Giles was a pious Christian, but nothing could be further from the truth. The explanation for the bowdlerising doubtless lies, rather, in Giles' Victorian background.

In point of fact, Giles outrightly rejected the historic Christianity of his Anglican Church. Giles' *Chinese Sketches* concludes with a chapter on 'Christianity'[191] in which he argues against missionary efforts in China, opines that the Chinese will never move in the direction of the Christian gospel, and ends his diatribe with his translation of a turgid, 'inflammatory placard, which was posted up last year at a place called Lung-p'ing, near the great tea mart of Hankow'.[192] These 'anti-Christian lyrics' include:

> Those who now embrace Christ
> Call him Lord of heaven and earth,
> Worshipping him with prayer,
> Deceiving and exciting the foolish,
> Dishonouring the holy teaching of Confucius.
> . . .
> I say unto you,
> And you should give heed unto me,
> Believe not the nonsense of Redemption,
> Believe not the trickery of the Resurrection.[193]

So why did Giles reject Christianity?

The final chapter of *Chinese Sketches* just referred to gives a hint: Giles is concerned with the question as to whether

Christianity would elevate the social morality of China beyond its present state, and he concludes, by comparing it with Western history, that it would not. Nowhere does he deal with *the truth issue*—whether Christianity is in fact *true* based on the historically verifiable, miraculous ministry of Jesus Christ.

Further insight comes from Giles' family experience. In the preface to the posthumous publication of Giles' 'Memoirs',[194] the editor writes:

> Herbert Allen Giles was born in Oxford on 18th December 1845, the fourth son of John Allen Giles (1808–84), an Anglican clergyman and Fellow of Corpus Christi College. His father had doctrinal differences with the Church and served a term in prison for a minor infraction of ecclesiastical law. As a consequence he was obliged to make ends meet with his pen, producing a stream of publications, many of a decidedly utilitarian nature, such as a series of 'cribs' of Greek and Latin texts for schoolboys. It was as a contributor to the latter that Herbert Giles made his earliest foray into the world of letters. His later agnosticism and anti-clericalism no doubt had their origins in his father's ordeal at the hands of the Church of England.[195]

Ecclesiastical bureaucracy and legalism were surely important factors in Herbert Giles' eventual rejection of Christianity.

But the Church cannot be entirely to blame. Giles' father was a nineteenth-century biblical liberal who did not believe that the gospel records were produced earlier than mid-second century! The Reverend John Allen Giles states in the preface to his *Christian Records on the Age, Authorship, and Authenticity of the Books of the New Testament* (1854) that the 'Gospels and Acts were not in existence before the year 150'. A reviewer of this work wrote: 'His [Giles] object is to establish—against Paley especially—a set of purely negative results; that the historical books of the New Testament are without any evidence, external or internal, of origin from an apostolical period or source; and abound in irreconcilable discrepancies.'[196]

With this kind of paternal history and theology, it becomes clearer why H. A. Giles preferred agnosticism.

Eduard Preuss

The translator of fundamental works of sixteenth- and seventeenth-century Lutheran orthodoxy, Eduard Preuss,[197] a professor at the Concordia Theological Seminary, St. Louis, Missouri, converted to Roman Catholicism toward the end of his life—having come to reject the fundamental Lutheran (and biblical!) teaching of salvation by grace alone through faith alone (*sola fide*).

How was such a radical conversion possible?

Professor Roland F. Ziegler of Concordia Seminary in Ft. Wayne, Indiana, has dealt with this question in detail in an important scholarly article,[198] and we shall benefit from his analysis:

> At the Friedrich-Wilhelm-Universität in Berlin as a *Privlltdazent* he was allowed to lecture but was not salaried. . . . Preuss's career came to a sudden halt when he was accused of improper relations with his pupils. He resigned from his position and, without any prospects in teaching, friends collected money for him to emigrate to America. There he was welcomed by the Missouri Synod after Karl Buchsel, the General Superintendent of Berlin, vouched for his innocence. He became a professor at Concordia

Seminary, St. Louis, and taught Church history, and Old and New Testament from 1869 till 1871. . . . At the end of 1871, Preuss suddenly resigned his position at the seminary; he was received into the Roman Catholic Church by baptism in early 1872. . . .

The only source for Preuss's reasons for defecting to Rome is the account he published seven years later. . . . The most prominent feature in Preuss's account was the experience of failure. What got him to doubt was the dissonance between his zealous defense of pure doctrine and the personal and professional disaster he experienced in Germany. The '*Lutheranergott*' ('god of the Lutherans'), as he called the deity, he worshipped when he was a Lutheran, a deity, as he stated, that was half-forgotten when Preuss had started to defend him, had allowed that his livelihood was destroyed. 'Truly, the god of the Lutherans has to be a completely impotent being, more impotent even than "the absolute Spirit" of the rationalists, of whose nullity the editor of Gerhard's *Loci* [i.e., Preuss] had previously made fun.'

Of course, Preuss knew that the Christians had suffered persecution before. But their persecutions had glorified God's cause and led to the conversion of many. Preuss's sufferings led not to the increase of the church, rather, the liberals triumphed-and that was it. There was no happy ending for him.

Preuss saw this story also repeated in the fate of the Lutheran Church. Of course, Preuss knew that the Christians had suffered persecution before. But their persecutions had glorified God's cause and led to the conversion of many. Elector John the Constant was incarcerated and lost most of his territory. The university he founded, Jena, had become a bulwark of the Enlightenment by the 19th century. The city of Magdeburg, our Lord's chancellery during the interim, was destroyed in 1631 by a Roman Catholic army, and there was no Lutheranism in it left at the time he wrote. Lutheranism in general had turned into pietism and rationalism and then into atheism. 'The poor god of the Lutherans had to watch calmly, as other, more powerful ones, robbed millions of his children.' Thus, it is the experience of God's absence and his perceived non-interference in the world, his experienced powerlessness, that made Preuss question his faith. The God whom Preuss experienced was a God who lacked the predicates of omnipotence and wisdom. In contrast to Lutheranism that was in shambles after three hundred years, stood the Roman Church, which was powerful, making converts, and was not riled by apostasy from the faith. Thus, behind Preuss's problems was the expectation that God's might is manifested in the preservation and growth of his church.

It is of course easy to condemn Preuss for thinking that he knew more about what God should have been doing providentially in history than God himself apparently knew. Clearly, Preuss did not realise that such reasoning was identical to that of the Enlightenment rationalists he found so obnoxious.

But on an even more fundamental level, one must look to the event that triggered Preuss' movement away from historic Lutheranism: the (apparently false) accusation against him of sexual impropriety that led his superiors to destroy his academic and theological career in Germany.

Conclusion

What do these two sad accounts of defection from biblical Christianity have in common?

There is, of course, the personal, psychological element—always present in conversions. But here, as in so many other such cases, there are objective considerations. First, the devastating role that rationalism and biblical criticism have played in the modern church from the eighteenth century to this very day and, secondly, the effect of the legalistic hurt that orthodox church bodies so often inflict on their leaders or tolerate by uncritically believing the worst concerning them.[199] 'My brethren, these things ought not so to be' (James 3:10).

CORONAVIRUS

If you are as sick as I am of receiving virus messages, you will have a tendency to trash this piece without even reading it. I'm not sure that I would blame you, but I hope you won't. For, *mirabile dictu*, it actually contains some serious theology.

When I wrote my book, *Human Rights and Human Dignity*,[200] I of course mentioned in passing philosophers of animal liberation such as John Aspinall, who suggested that the world might be better off sans people. One wonders if, at the moment, Aspinall and company are keeping track of their own viral state . . .

Even serious theological operations have been sending messages that boil down to (1) this is an unprecedented situation, (2) we can't explain it but need to hang in there through courage and prayer, (3) we must maintain family values, (4) don't forget to wash your hands continually, and (5) the authorities are doing all they can.

Now, I may be wrong, but is there anything non-platitudinous here? Anything that even low-IQ Christian believers would not have thought of on their own?

But then we also receive from these same organisations additional monetary appeals. For example, one such group points out, that, as always, it is holding high Sola Gratia, whilst virtually all evangelicals think that their salvation is dependent, as least in part, on their personal faith-efforts. So send us another contribution!

We seem to hear Dr. Newby Faustus (Ph.D. from an English minor provincial university, a former polytechnic, that requires no language or comprehensive examinations, but which accepted his thesis *in camera* on 'Law-Gospel Teaching in the Book of Ecclesiasticus'). Here we overhear Faustus in conversation with one of the writers of this infinite stream of coronavirus appeals:

> Excellent series of email messages to your constituency! You never talk above their heads and you properly treat them like children who need single-syllable instruction during their first week in Sunday school. You tell them nothing that they haven't already heard more than once through the media and by way of emails from similar organisations. You have succeeded in reinforcing the obvious—if not ad infinitum, surely ad nauseam.
>
> Particularly impressive is your total avoidance of the key questions an unbeliever would be desperately asking: If there is a good God, *why*? Why one person's financial collapse and not his neighbour's? Why this individual's survival but not that individual's? Why the death of medical personnel attempting to treat the critically ill?
>
> Especially helpful is your stress on your organisation's solid theology—offered as a corrective to those benighted evangelicals who suppose that their "decisions" to accept God's overwhelming sacrifice on the cross has had anything at all to do with their becoming genuine member of Christ's saving church.

So much for Faustus.

But what *can* be said with a minimum of banality and triteness concerning the current crisis—together with theology's place in the picture?

The Virus in Depth

The only possible ultimate explanation of *any* cosmic phenomenon would, by definition, have to come from a Divine Source. No Source, no explanation. A silent Source, likewise, would mean zero explanation. But the God who sent his Son Christ to save us has provided a written revelation, the Bible, declaring that the Creation was originally made perfect and was subsequently corrupted, physically and spiritually, by the perverse selfishness of God's creatures, who used their God-given freewill for their own advantage.

Result: A world in which evil / sin / dog-eat-dog selfishness runs rampant—and not in a predictable, rational fashion (the good living long and well, the nasty consistently being run over by freight trains)—and where the spillover effects of a fallen world often mean that there seems to be no one-on-one correlation at all among the causes and the effects of misery.

At the same time, the God of the Bible did not leave a fallen race in irrationality. We retain the rational ability to analyse the causes of specific evils and to employ our mental faculties to correct them. Thus the history of human progress in all spheres of life, including, and perhaps especially, in the areas of disease and medicine. Pasteur's discoveries in the nineteenth century are a glowing triumph of the application of God-given rationality to hideous, almost-universally misunderstood contemporary epidemics.

So now, from theology to plague: Where did today's coronavirus contagion arise?

COVID-19 is not the first coronavirus to appear. The current version surfaced in the Wuhan region of China at the end of 2019. A study published in March 2020 offered the sobering conclusion that if the totalitarian Chinese authorities had admitted the problem and begun containment measures just three weeks earlier than they did, the number of cases could have been reduced by 95 per cent, and its geographic spread (now present in more than seventy countries worldwide) could have been radically limited.[201]

The reputable journal *Nature Medicine* identifies the virus as a 'natural' phenomenon in a fallen world, not as something artificial or explicable as some kind of bizarre conspiracy theory resulting from genetic engineering. Two theories as to how the current plague began have been offered, and one of these seems well worth mentioning here, though it is clearly in need of further research.

Specialists have focused on several characteristic features of the SARS-CoV-2 virus, including the genetic template for spike proteins, armatures on the outside of the virus that it uses to grab and penetrate the outer walls of human and animal cells. If one considers the overall molecular structure of the SARS-CoV-2 virus, its 'backbone' resembles, though is not identical to, that already found in known coronaviruses, especially varieties found in bats.

In previous coronavirus outbreaks, humans have contracted the virus after direct exposure to civets (SARS) and camels (MERS). As a consequence, some researchers have proposed bats as the most likely reservoir for SARS-CoV-2, since it is very similar to a bat coronavirus. True, there are no documented cases of direct bat-human transmission, but there is no reason to ignore the existence of an intermediate host between bats and humans.

Chinese Folklore

In Chinese traditional folklore and religious symbolism, the bat could hardly be regarded more highly. It is a major representation of happiness and bliss. The bat-bliss connection, however, is not due to the inherent meaning of the words but rather to mere sound-play. Though the traditional characters for *bat* and *happiness* are entirely unrelated, their *sounds* (*fú*) are alike, as can be seen in the Pinyin romanised

蝙蝠   福
chauve·souris (biān fú) = bonheur (fú)

transcription system. Two bats facing each other in a decorative design will mean 'double bliss'. Five bats around a circle signify long life, riches, health, love of virtue, and a natural death. A red bat is a particularly beneficent sign, since the colour red has the capacity to drive away demons—and the pronunciation of the adjective *red* has the sound of the word *immense* (hóng). A rebus consisting of a bat with a valuable coin speaks of great fortune.

Considering the number of coronavirus deaths, it is interesting that in Chinese art and tradition, the bat is also a symbol of longevity. A sixteenth-century Chinese classic, *The Book of Plant Medicines*, claimed that the bat lived to a very great age, and that its blood, gallbladder, and wings have curative properties, improve the eyesight, and extend the life span.[202]

Conclusion: Good/Bad Science, Good/Bad Theology

General Douglas MacArthur had wanted to achieve a full-scale military defeat of Communist China. That might have been a gross tactical blunder, but had it successfully occurred rather than being deep-sixed politically, the Cultural Revolution with its human miseries would never have occurred, Tiananmen Square would be a historical non-event, and science might well have triumphed over the coronavirus bat and all its works and all its ways. And the Christian gospel itself might have become the dominant religious force in today's China.

But we are not prophets, nor the sons of prophets.

Our question to ourselves can only be *What should be the Christian's task during times of crisis?*

> First, we must substitute solid rationality for suspicion, ungrounded tradition, and wish fulfilment when making religious and scientific judgements.

> Secondly, we must not imagine that by expressing sermonic platitudes of sweetness and light, our hearers and readers will somehow be better off.

> Thirdly, we do not have the luxury of repeating mantras of the Reformation as if, like Chinese pictographs, they had the built-in power to achieve what a genuine, personal conviction of Christ's work at the cross—and that alone—can in fact achieve.

> Fourthly, *all* of Holy Scripture is *God-breathed*, and 'we know'—though there is no such promise to unbelievers—'that all things work together for good to them that love God, to them who are the called according to his purpose' (Rom 8:28).

> Finally (fifth bat?), there is absolutely no substitute for the Bible's ending prayer, to be uttered without ceasing: 'Even so, come, Lord Jesus' (Rev 22:20).

ARE CORONAVIRUS RESTRICTIONS ILLEGAL?

We have all been suffering from restricted movement, limited travel, and confinement. Have these governmental decisions been in fact illegal and unconstitutional?

A recent web article by a Tennessee lawyer[203] argues that this is indeed the case. His position, in his own words, is as follows: 'No one in the federal government, state government, or local government has any authority to dictate to the general public that they must stay home or that they must suspend their business, or that they must refrain from traveling, or that they must not gather together in large groups, etc. . . . Government was not instituted to protect our health; it was instituted to protect our *liberties*'.[204]

I do not know if the author is a card-carrying Libertarian, but this would fit perfectly in the context of that political philosophy. Some years ago, when I was teaching in a law school in Washington State, I was invited to the Tacoma Club by the Libertarian dean, who would have eliminated all licensing of professions—on the ground that government should always be restrained and should be focused almost solely on protecting civil liberties. I asked him about brain surgeons; his reply was that the poor ones would be forced out of business by the good ones. He was blithely unaware, apparently, of the harm to be caused by the unlicensed brain surgeons.

To be sure, as the old adage has it, 'the best government is the government that governs least'. But there will always be a need for governments to offer positive assistance to the needy in the populace. This is why most civilised states have some form of socialised medicine, and why it is most unfortunate that, in the case of the United States, the Democrats finally achieved 'Obama care'—in the absence of a Republican, and therefore more economically responsible, programme to provide needed medical assistance beyond the means of so many of the citizenry.

In Chinese mythology, there is the 獬豸 (xièzhì) unicorn who is mentioned as early as the Han Dynasty. A scholar of the time described him as a 'righteous beast, which rams the wrongful party when it hears an argument'.[205] I believe that he would have given a severe butt to the author of the above-quoted article.[206]

Why? American constitutional law has always permitted loss to individuals when not allowing this would produce immense suffering to others. The classic example is the permissible destruction of property to create firebreaks in the face of raging forest fires (as in California).[207] To be sure, the owners of the destroyed property must receive compensation, but the destruction per se is by no means constitutionally prohibited.

And what about seat-belt regulations for drivers of motor vehicles? Legally required helmets for motorcyclists? Mandatory insurance for those who operate cars or motorcycles on public highways? Standards of cleanliness for restaurants? All of these regulations impose a burden on the few for the sake of the many—even when the only harm might be to the individual himself or herself.

Sir William Blackstone, in the first textbook of English common law, argued that suicide should be criminalised because the subject did not live in isolation; he owed a duty to his Sovereign:

> The law of England wisely and religiously considers, that no man hath a power to destroy life, but by commission from God, the author of it: and, as the suicide is guilty of a double offence; one spiritual, in invading the prerogative of the Almighty, and rushing into his immediate presence uncalled for; the other temporal, against the king, who hath an interest in the preservation of all his subjects.[208]

The essential point here is that no individual is a Robinson Crusoe, living in isolation from others (and even Crusoe had his man Friday). John Donne gave classic expression to the truth that we are all interlocked with others; we all owe a responsibility to those around us in society: on hearing the bell toll announcing the death of someone, 'Never send to know / for whom the bell tolls, / it tolls for thee.'

So we have no choice but to suffer in the wake of the coronavirus—masks, confinement, limited travel, etc. One would think that the biblical perspective that we are to serve as 'our brother's keeper' (Gen 4:9) ought to encourage at least Christian believers to think theologically instead of in Libertarian terms. After all, the Bible comes from God himself, whereas political philosophies are but the work of limited, finite, sinful human beings.

PUNISHMENT AND WORKS-RIGHTEOUSNESS

'The Husband Punished' is one of the delightful *Strange Stories from a Chinese Studio*. The editor and translator, H. A. Giles, adds the following note near the end of the tale:

> The virtuous conduct of any individual will result not only in happiness and prosperity to himself, but a certain quantity of these will descend to his posterity, unless, as in the present case, there is one among them whose personal wickedness neutralizes any benefits that would otherwise accrue therefrom. Here we have an instance where the crimes of a descendant still left a balance of good fortune surviving from the accumulated virtue of generations.[209]

Is this close to biblical teaching as set forth in such Old Testament passages Exodus 34:6–7, Leviticus 26:39, and Deuteronomy 5:8–10? *Hardly.*

After noting other scriptural passages that seem to present a different approach (Deuteronomy 24:16, 2 Kings 14:5, Ezekiel 18:20), John Piper argues two points: (1) 'The sins of the fathers are punished in the children *through becoming the sins of the children*', and (2) 'Because of God's grace, which is finally secured by Christ, the children can confess their own sins and the sins of their fathers and be forgiven and be accepted by God.'[210]

Note, furthermore—and especially—that the Chinese view embraces both punishment *and merit*: 'accumulated virtue'.

At the very heart of the biblical teaching of salvation lies the truth, expressly set forth in Ephesians 2:8–9: 'By grace are ye saved through faith; and that not of yourselves: it is the gift of God: not of works, lest any man should boast.' This is, to be sure, the source of the fundamental teaching of the Protestant Reformation: salvation by grace alone, through faith alone, as revealed in the Holy Scriptures alone: *sola gratia, sola fide, sola scriptura*.

What principally distinguishes Christianity from all the other world's religions, including Taoism, Confucianism, and Buddhism? *The way of salvation*, offered in Holy Writ as a free gift through the sacrifice of Christ, God's Son, for the sins of the whole world.

NOTES

1. Fax reproduced photographically in *ACTUEL: Chine. Dix ans d'une revolution qui n'est pas finie* (hors serie, 1989), pp. 78–79 In fact, the number of persons killed probably did not exceed three thousand—still, of course, a horrendous number, 'It is now generally accepted that most of the killings in the crackdown took place not in the square but on the northside, along the Avenue of Eternal Peace, and in other parts of the city' (*The New York Times*, 14 April 1990). See also *People's Republic of China: Preliminary Findings on Killings of Unarmed Civilians, Arbitrary Arrests and Summary Executions since June 3 1989* (New York: Amnesty International, August 1989); Amnesty estimates civilian deaths as 'at least a thousand'.

    The French journal ACTUEL has been at the forefront in supporting the Chinese prodemocracy movement. In its issue of 19 March 1990, *Newsweek* reported under the rubric 'Radio Free China' (p. 34): 'Somewhere off the Chinese coast next month, a radio station aboard an ageing cargo ship renamed the Goddess of Democracy will start beaming uncensored radio into the People's Republic. Radio Voice of Democracy in China, sponsored by the French monthly *Actuel*, will feature news bulletins and rock music. It will broadcast messages from Chinese exiles. And it will have a call-in phone line, so Chinese on the mainland can go on the air, too. "The Chinese woke the world in 1989. In 1990 they're alone," says French journalist Christophe Nick, who conceived the project. "They shouldn't be forgotten."

    'Unlike short-wave stations like Voice of America and the BBC World Service, the Voice of Democracy in China will be medium wave—receivable even on rudimentary transistor radios. A high-power transmitter aboard ship and relay stations near Chinese borders should be able to evade jamming, Nick says, and ensure that the signal can be picked up from Tibet to Inner Mongolia. (It will operate in a variety of Chinese dialects.) So far, the Goddess of Democracy, which left the coast of France last week, has enough cash from donations to keep afloat till mid-June. A multilingual version of John Lennon's "Imagine" will go on sale in May to raise additional funds. Nick, who was in Tiananmen Square during the crackdown last June, hopes for enough to last until the year-end. "This is not some pirate counterpropaganda thing," says Nick. "This is . . . a free-press radio."'

2. *Massacre in Beijing: China's Struggle for Democracy*, by the Editors of Time Magazine and ed. by Donald Morrison (New York: Warner Books, 1989), pp. 259–61. See also the impressionistic and personal story collection by Bette Bao Lord, *Legacies: A Chinese Mosaic* (New York: Knopf, 1990).

3. See John Warwick Montgomery, *The Quest for Noah's Ark* (rev. ed.; Minneapolis: Bethany, 1974).

4. Montgomery, 'A Day in East German Luther Country', in his *In Defense of Martin Luther* (Milwaukee: Northwestern Publishing House, 1970), pp. 150–58.

5. *China: An Introduction*, ed. Qi Wen (Beijing: Foreign Languages Press, 1984), p. 1.

6. *China Daily*, 9 June 1989, p. 1.

7. Ed Plowman, *Billy Graham in China* (Minneapolis: Billy Graham Evangelistic Association, 1988), pp. 44–46 (with an excellent photograph of the chapel where Dr. Montgomery spoke).

8. *China Daily* [Beijing], 2 June 1989, p. 1.

9. *China Daily* [Beijing], 3 June 1989, p. 1.

10. *China Daily* [Beijing], 6 June 1989, p. 1.

11. *China Daily* [Beijing], 8 June 1989, p. 1. On the Chinese government's disinformation campaign, see *The Year of the Lie: Censorship and Disinformation in the People's Republic of China 1989* (London: Article 19, 1989); reviewed in *Human Rights Quarterly*, XII/1 (February 1990), pp. 179–80.

12. Quoted in Robina Gibb, 'Hong Kong's Future Shock; The Realities of 1997', *Newsweek*, 5 June 1989, p. 12. See also Joel Kotkin, 'Preparing for the Worst, Hong Kong Expects Best', *The Los Angeles Times*, 8 April 1990; and Nicholas D. Kristof, 'In Hong Kong, A Deepening Sense of Despair and Betrayal', *The New York Times*, 23 April 1990.

13. 'We Love Rice, but We Love Democracy More' (Anthony Shang, producer/director), Channel 4 Television, London, England, 21 August 1989.

14. Quoted (in French translation) in *Le Point*, 29 May 1989, p. 28.

15. Marguerite Johnson, 'Condemnation—with Caution', *Time* Magazine, 19 June 1989, pp. 26-27.

16. See Montgomery, *Human Rights & Human* (Richardson, Texas: Probe, 1986), p. 276.

17. 334 U.S. 1, 3 A.L.R. 2d, 441 (1948).

18. William F. Buckley, 'Protect Chinese Students from Peking' (nationally syndicated), *The Morning News Tribune* (Tacoma, WA), 29 November 1989.

19. Lewis M. Simons (Knight-Ridder Newspapers), *The Orange County Register*, 16 June 1989.

20. Lewis M. Simons, *The Orange County Register*, 19 June 1989.

21. See Montgomery, *The Shape of the Past* (rev. ed.; Minneapolis: Bethany, 1975), p. 9.

22. Catherine Sampson (Beijing), *The Times* (London), 23 June 1989.

23. Nicholas D. Kristof (New York Times Service), *The International Herald Tribune*, 24-25 June 1989. What is the fate of the student activists almost a year later? Little is known, but two student leaders on the 'most wanted' list were able to escape to France after ten months in hiding (*The New York Times*, 8 and 14 April 1990). See also, Sheryl Wu Dunn, 'The Prisoners of Tiananmen Square', *The New York Times Magazine*, 8 April 1990, pp. 29-34 (on six of the demonstrators).

24. *The Orange County Register*, 24 August 1989 (from *The New York Times*).

25. David Holley, *The Los Angeles Times*, 28 August 1989.

26. David Holley, *The Los Angeles Times*, 5 September 1989.

27. *The Times-Picayune*, 16 October 1989 (from the Associated Press).

28. Mark O'Neill (Reuters), *The Orange County Register*, 23 October 1989.

29. George Lardner, Jr. (Washington Post), *The Morning News Tribune* (Tacoma, WA), 13 December 1989.

30. Ron Redmond, *The Seattle Times/Seattle Post-Intelligencer*, 21 February 1990.

31. Tom Brown, *The Seattle Times/Seattle Post-Intelligencer*, 4 March 1990.

32. *The Seattle Times/Seattle Post-Intelligencer*, 13 March 1990 (from Reuters).

33. *The Seattle Times/Seattle Post-Intelligencer*, 18 March 1990 (from the Associated Press).

34. *The Seattle Times/Seattle Post-Intelligencer*, 21 March 1990 (from the Associated Press).

35. George Catlin, *The Story of the Political Philosophers* (New York and London: Whittlesey House, 1939), p. 569.

36. George H. Sabine, *A History of Political Theory* (New York: Henry Holt, 1937), p. 637.

37. *Ibid.*, p. 642.

38. Vernon Venable, *Human Nature: The Marxian View* (New York: Alfred A. Knopf, 1946), p. 37.

39. Karl Marx and Friedrich Engels, *The German Ideology, Parts I and III*, ed. R. Pascal (New York: International Publishers, 1939), pp. 28–29.

40. Engels, at the annual conference of the German Socialists (quoted in Catlin, *op. cit.*, pp. 578–79).

41. 'The proletariat . . . is compelled as proletariat to abolish itself, and therewith to abolish private property, the opposite that has determined its own existence, that has made it into a proletariat' (Karl Marx, *The Holy Family*; quoted in Catlin, *op. cit.*, p. 593).

42. See section IV of Marx' *Critique of the Gotha Programme* (in his *Selected Works*, ed. V. Adoratsky (2 vols.; New York: International Publishers, n.d.), II, pp. 576–80).

43. On this aspect of Marxian theory, see Keith McDonald's excellent article, 'Marxism; An Analysis and Criticism', *HIS* (InterVarsity Christian Fellowship), December 1947, pp. 6–13.

44. Karl Marx and Friedrich Engels, *The Communist Manifesto* (New York: International Publishers, 1948), p. 44.

45. K. Campbell, 'Materialism', in *The Encyclopedia of Philosophy*, ed. Paul Edwards (8 vols.; New York: Macmillan & The Free Press; London: Collier-Macmillan, 1967), V, p. 184.

46. Montgomery, *The Shape of the Past* (*op. cit.*); *Where Is History Going? Essays in Support of the Historical Truth of Christian Revelation* (reprint ed.; Minneapolis: Bethany, 1972); *The Law Above the Law* (Minneapolis: Bethany, 1975); *Faith Founded on Fact* (Nashville and New York: Thomas Nelson, 1978); *Human Rights & Human Dignity* (*op. cit.*), chap. 6. On the case for God's existence, see Montgomery, 'Is Man His Own God?', in his *Christianity for the Toughminded* (Minneapolis: Bethany, 1973), pp. 21–34. *Where Is History Going?* is available in German under the title *Weltgeschichte wohin?* (Neuhausen-Stuttgart: Haenssler-Verlag, 1977).

47. M. S. McDougal, H. D. Lasswell, and Lung-chu Chen, *Human Rights and World Public Order* (New Haven and London: Yale University Press, 1980), p. 79.

48. Montgomery, 'Progressivistic Mirage', in his *The Shaping of America* (Minneapolis: Bethany, 1976), pp. 69–87.

49. McDougal, Lasswell, and Chen, *loc. cit.*

50. Karl Löwith, *Meaning in History* (Chicago: University of Chicago Press Phoenix Books, 1957), p. 43.

51. G. Smith, 'Marxian Metaphysics and Individual Freedom', in G. H. R. Parkinson (ed.), *Marx and Marxisms* (Cambridge; Cambridge University Press, 1982), pp. 241–42.

52. *Cf.* Francis Nigel Lee, *Communist Eschatology* (Nutley, New Jersey: Craig Press, 1974). Erickson, following Clark Williamson, identifies 'sixteen points on which the Marxist and biblical-prophetic interpretations of history coincide.

These are; 1) history has a meaning of its own; 2) history has an aim, an end, a beginning and a centre; 3) the content of history is the fight between the forces of good and evil; 4) each is characterised by an eschatological mood; 5) each arises as an attack on an existing order; 6) each believes that the transition to a new order will occur only by the medium of a catastrophic event of events; 7) each seeks the establishment of a kingdom of peace and justice; 8) each thinks the kingdom is at hand; 9) each regards certain minority groups as the bearers of historical destiny (poor, slaves, etc); 10) each posits that man is not what he ought to be but is fallen and estranged; 11) each regards man as an historical social being; 12) each defines truth in terms of the union of theory and practice, i.e., truth must be done; 13) each holds that only the elect can know the truth; 14) each mounts a protest against idols or ideology; 15) each thinks salvation is possible and inevitable; 16) each looks for the coming of a new man or a new creature'—Nancy Erickson, 'Theory and Practice in Contemporary Marxism: A Christian Response' (essay presented at the 13th Fall Meeting of the Conference on Faith and History, Terre Haute, Indiana, 11-13 November 1982), p. 23.

53. Eric Voegelin, *Order and History* (4 vols.; Baton Rouge: Louisiana State University Press, 1956 to date), III, p. 278; *cf.* his *The New Science of Politics* (Chicago and London: University of Chicago Press, 1952). It should be noted that Voegelin also condemns the West for equal but opposite *metastatic gnosis* in believing that the individualistic 'American way of life' is the route to Utopia.

54. See Thomas Molnar, *Utopia, the Perennial Heresy* (New York; Sheed & Ward, 1972); and *cf.* Montgomery, 'The Millennium', in *The International Standard Bible Encyclopedia*, ed. Geoffrey W. Bromiley (rev. ed., 4 vols.; Grand Rapids, Michigan: Eerdmans, 1986), III, pp. 356-61.

55. Jack Higgins, *Solo* (London: Collins Pan Books, 1981), p. 116.

56. Valery Chalidze, *To Defend These Rights: Human Rights and the Soviet Union*, trans. Guy Daniels (New York; Random House, 1974). pp. 7-8.

57. G. Brunner, 'Communist Analysis of Fundamental Rights', in *Marxism, Communism and Western Society: A Comparative*

Encyclopedia, ed. C. D. Kernig (4 vols.; New York: Herder and Herder, 1972), IV, pp. 62, 64.

58. Cornelius Murphy, 'Ideological Interpretations of Human Rights', *DePaul Law Review*, XXI/2 (1971), pp. 304–5. For a detailed analysis of the Marxist system vis-a-vis human rights, see Montgomery, *The Marxist Approach to Human Rights: Analysis & Critique*, published as Vol. III (1983–1984) of *The Simon Greenleaf Law Review*; material in the preceding sections of the present chapter has been derived in large part from this work.

59. *China: An Introduction* (*op. cit.*), p. 15.

60. Arthur A. Cohen, *The Communism of Mao Tse-tung* (Chicago and London: University of Chicago Press, 1964), pp. 189–90.

61. The phraseology comes from Ross Terrill, *800,000,000: The Real China* (Boston: Little, Brown, 1972), especially pp. 218–26.

62. *China: An Introduction* (*op. cit.*), pp. 26–27.

63. Eileen Donahoe, 'The Promise of Law for the Post-Mao Leadership of China', *Stanford Law Review*, XLI (November, 1988), p. 172.

64. *Ibid.*, pp. 179, 184.

65. *The Laws of the People's Republic of China 1979–1982*, compiled by the Legislative Affairs Commission of the Standing Committee of the National People's Congress of the People's Republic of China (Beijing: Foreign Languages Press, 1987), p. 103.

66. Mikhail Gorbachev, *Perestroika: New Thinking for Our Country and the World* (New York: Harper & Row, 1987), pp. 17, 24–25, 31, 56, 139, 143.

67. Rong Zhi and Zhang Wuzhuan, 'Gorbachev's "New Thinking" and Foreign Policy Adjustments', in *China on World Affairs 2* (Beijing: Beijing Review, 1989), p. 66.

68. John King Fairbank, *The United States and China* (rev. ed.; New York: Viking Press, 1962), p. 97 (italics ours).

69. Kenneth Scott Latourette, *The Chinese: Their History and Culture* (4th ed.; New York: Macmillan; London: Collier-Macmillan, 1964), pp. 523–24.

70. Michael Loewe, *Everyday Life in Early Imperial China* (New York: Dorset Press, 1988), pp. 108-9.

71. Jonathan Chamberlain, *Chinese Gods* (Selangor Darul Ehsan, Malaysia: Pelanduk Publications, 1987), p. 40.

72. *Ibid.*, pp. 41-43.

73. Valentine Rodolphe Burkhardt, *Chinese Creeds & Customs* (3 vols.; Hong Kong: South China Morning Post, 1972), II, pp. 143-45.

74. Latourette, *op. cit.*, p. 551.

75. See Montgomery, 'China, India, and Tibet', in his *Principalities and Powers: The World of the Occult* (Minneapolis: Bethany, 1973), pp. 49-50.

76. Latourette, *op. cit.*, p. 555.

77. Burkhardt, *op. cit.*, I, pp. 122-23.

78. Latourette, *op. cit.*, pp. 554-55.

79. *Ibid.*, pp. 553-54 (italics ours).

80. C. K. Yang, 'The Functional Relationship Between Confucian Thought and Chinese Religion', in *Chinese Thought and Institutions*, ed. John King Fairbank (Chicago and London: University of Chicago Press, 1957), p. 290.

81. See Montgomery, *History & Christianity* (*op. cit.*), and *Where Is History Going?* (*op. cit.*).

82. Robert Ernest Hume, *The World's Living Religions* (rev. ed.; New York; Scribner, 1941), p. 131.

83. Basel: Missionsbuchhandlung, 1914.

84. C. S. Lewis, *The Abolition of Man* (New York: Macmillan, 1947), pp. 51-61. *Cf.* Montgomery, *Human Rights & Human Dignity* (*op. cit.*), pp. 122 ff.

85. Quoted from manuscript by Janwillem Van de Wetering, *Robert Van Gulik: His Life, His Work* (Miami Beach, Florida: Dennis McMillan Publications, 1987), pp. 13-14.

86. Hume, *op. cit.*, pp. 143-44.

87. Joseph Needham, *Science and Civilization in China*, Vol. II: *History of Scientific Thought* (Cambridge: Cambridge

University Press, 1956), p. 556. *Cf.* also Needham's *Science in Traditional China* (Cambridge, Mass: Harvard University Press; Hong Kong: Chinese University Press, 1981).

88. Ted J. Kaptchuk, *The Web That Has No Weaver: Understanding Chinese Medicine* (New York; Congdon & Weed, 1983), pp. 257-58, 264-65. Kaptchuk is a Doctor of Oriental Medicine and of the Jewish persuasion. On the important contribution of Reformation theology to the rise of science in Western Europe in the 17th century, see Montgomery, *Cross and Crucible* (2 vols.; 'International Archives of the History of Ideas', 55; The Hague, Netherlands: Martinus Nijhoff, 1973).

89. Hume, *op. cit.*, pp. 129-30.

90. The most helpful recent edition is *The Analects*, ed. and trans. D. C. Lau (New York: Dorset Press, 1986).

91. Y. C. Yang, *China's Religious Heritage* (New York and Nashville: Abingdon-Cokesbury, 1943), p. 63.

92. Montgomery, *Human Rights & Human Dignity* (*op. cit.*), p. 97.

93. Robert Paul Wolff, *Understanding Rawls: A Reconstruction and Critique of. 'A Theory of Justice'* (Princeton, New Jersey: Princeton University Press, 1977), p. 111.

94. H. G. Creel, *Chinese Thought from Confucius to Mao* (New York: New American Library Mentor Books, 1960), chap. 7 ('The Authoritarianism of Hsun Tzu'), pp. 98 ff.

95. Yang, *op. cit.*, pp. 80-83.

96. Hume, *op. cit.*, p. 119.

97. Donald J. Munro, *The Concept of Man in Early China* (Stanford, California: Stanford University Press, 1969), p. vii.

98. Yang, *op. cit.*, p. 83.

99. James Legge, 'Confucius', *Encyclopaedia Britannica*, 11th ed. (1910-1911), VI, p. 912. Legge wrote, inter alia. *The Life and Teaching of Confucius* (1867), *Life and Teaching of Mencius* (1875), and *The Religions of China* (1880).

100. Edward J. Thomas, *The Life of Buddha As Legend and History* (New York: Barnes & Noble, 1956), p. 251.

101. Hume, *op. cit.*, pp. 612.

102. Irving Alan Sparks, 'Buddha and Christ: A Functional Analysis', *Numen*, XIII (October, 1966), p. 195.

103. *Living Buddhism in Japan*, ed. Yoshiro Tamura (Tokyo: International Institute for the Study of Religions, 1960), chap. 8 ('Buddha and the Pure Land'), p. 49.

104. E. Steinilber-Oberlin (with the collaboration of Kuni Matsuo), *The Buddhist Sects of Japan: Their History, Philosophical Doctrines and Sanctuaries*, trans. Marc Logé (London: George Allen & Unwin, 1938), pp. 190–91, 202 (italics ours).

105. Tucker N. Callaway, *Japanese Buddhism and Christianity: A Comparison of the Christian Doctrine of Salvation with that of some Major Sects of Japanese Buddhism* (Tokyo: Shinkyo Shuppansha, 1957), pp. 104–10.

106. Hume, *op. cit.*, p. 75.

107. Yang, *op. cit.*, p. 121.

108. See Montgomery, *Christianity for the Toughminded* (*op. cit.*), pp. 145–55.

109. Hume, *op. cit.*, p. 69. Buddhists themselves have been sadly incapable of rehabilitating their religion from such criticisms; see, for example, D. T. Suzuki, *Buddhist Philosophy and Its Effects on the Life and Thought of the Japanese People* (Tokyo: Society for International Cultural Relations, 1936). On the human-rights failing of Eastern religions, see Montgomery, *Human Rights & Human Dignity* (*op. cit.*), pp. 112 ff.

110. Arthur Koestler, *The Lotus and the Robot* (New York: Macmillan, 1961), especially pp. 236–41, 268–75. Tragically, Koestler's personal search for truth never brought him to the cross of Christ; he and his wife ultimately died in a suicide pact.

111. Latourette, *op. cit.*, p. 526.

112. *Ibid.*, p. 528.

113. Kurt Baier, *The Moral Point of View* (New York: Random House, 1965), p. 157.

114. See also Wittgenstein's posthumously published 'A Lecture on Ethics', *Philosophical Review*, LXXIV (January, 1965); and *cf.* Montgomery, *The Suicide of Christian Theology* (Minneapolis: Bethany, 1971), pp. 364–66.

115. For the text of Solzhenitsyn's 1970 Nobel Prize lecture, see *The New York Times*, 30 September 1972. *Cf.* Niels C. Nielsen, Jr., *Solzhenitzyn's Religion* (Nashville and New York: Thomas Nelson, 1975).

116. See, in general, Kenneth Scott Latourette, *A History of Christian Missions in China* (New. York: Macmillan, 1929); and Jessie G. Lutz (ed.), *Christian Missions in China: Evangelists of What?* ('Problems in Asian Civilizations'; Boston: D. C. Heath, 1965).

117. 'Monothelites' held that the incarnate Christ had only one will rather than both a divine and a human will.

118. *The Travels of Marco Polo*, ed. E. Dennison Ross and Eileen Power (London: Routledge, 1931), p. 6, iii f.

119. For valuable insight into Ricci's approach, see Martin Jarrett-Kerr, *Patterns of Christian Acceptance: Individual Response to the Missionary Impact, 1550–1950* (London: Oxford University Press, 1972), pp. 50 ff.

120. WA, 23, 645, 30. For a full discussion of this subject, see Montgomery, 'Luther and the Missionary Challenge', in his *In Defense of Martin Luther* (Milwaukee: Northwestern Publishing House, 1970), pp. 159–69.

121. On Morrison, see J. Theodore Mueller, *Great Missionaries to China* (Grand Rapids, Michigan: Zondervan, n.d.), pp. 39 ff.

122. J. Leclercq, *La Vie du Père Lebbe* (Paris, 1961), pp. 81–82.

123. Paul A. Cohen, *China and Christianity: The Missionary Movement and the Growth of Chinese Anti-foreignism, 1860–1870* (Cambridge, Mass: Harvard University Press, 1963), p. 45.

124. On Griffith John, see Mueller, *op. cit.*, pp. 119 ff., and R. Wardlaw Thompson, *Griffith John: The Story of Fifty Years in China* (London, 1908).

125. *Pi-hsieh chi-shih* (1871 ed.), *chuan-hsia*, pp. 13a-b, 17b.

126. Many other great names could of course also be mentioned if space permitted—for example, Go forth of China, John and Betty Stam, and Dr. William J. Boone (on the latter, see Muriel Boone, *The Seed of the Church in China* [Edinburgh: Saint Andrew Press, 1973]).

127. The standard biography is *Hudson Taylor and the China Inland Mission* by Dr. and Mrs. Howard Taylor (London:' Religious Tract Society, 1940). See also J. Hudson Taylor's autobiographical *Retrospect* (3rd ed.; Philadelphia and Toronto: China Inland Mission, n.d.).

128. Quoted in Mueller, *op. cit.*, pp. 110–12.

129. Clifton J. Phillips, 'The Student Volunteer Movement and Its Role in China Missions, 1886–1920', in John King Fairbank (ed.). *The Missionary Enterprise in China and America* (Cambridge, Mass: Harvard University Press, 1974), pp. 95–96.

130. Marshall Broomhall, *The Jubilee Story of the China Inland Mission* (Philadelphia and Toronto: China Inland Mission, 1915), p. 169.

131. On the history of the China Inland Mission, see especially M. G. Guinness, *Story of the China Ireland Mission* (2 vols.; London, 1893); Marshall Broomhall, *Faith and Facts As Illustrated in the History of the China Inland Mission* (London, 1909); and Leslie T. Lyall, *A Passion for the Impossible: The China Inland Mission, 1865–1965* (Chicago: Moody Press, 1965).

132. M. Searle Bates, 'The Theology of American Missionaries in China, 1900–1950', in John King Fairbank (ed.). *The Missionary Enterprise in China and America* (*op. cit.*), pp. 142–43.

133. Phillips, *op. cit.*, p. 102.

134. See D. P. Thomson, *Eric H. Liddell, Athlete and Missionary* (rev. ed.; Barnoak, Crieff, Perthshire, Scotland: The Research Unit, 1971). This is the definitive biography, with full bibliography; an earlier edition appeared under the title, *Scotland's Greatest Athlete*.

135. David J. Michell, 'I Remember Eric Liddell', in *The Disciplines of the Christian Life* by Eric Liddell (London: Triangle/SPCK, 1985), pp. 11–12.

136. Latourette, *A History of Christian Missions in China* (*op. cit.*), p. 407.

137. These statistics derive from: Allen J. Swanson, *Taiwan: Mainline Versus Independent Church Growth* (South Pasadena, California: William Carey Library, 1970), p. 283.

138. Alan F. Gates, *Think China: A Study Book on China* (Pasadena, California: William Carey Library, 1979), p. 48. Gates quotes Arthur Glasses unpublished study, 'Success and Failure in the China Mission' (Consultation of Missions to China and the Chinese, March, 1975).

139. The Communist plan of de-christianising China is known from an official publication offering advice to Cuban leaders so that they can succeed along the same lines. See Li Weihan, 'Christian and Crisis', *The Catholic Church and Cuba: Programme for Action* (13 May 1968). The author was a close associate of Chou En-lai from 1949 to 1959.

140. Richard C. Bush, Jr., *Religion in Communist China* (New York and Nashville: Abingdon, 1970), p. 275.

141. Jiang Zhimin, 'Neubelebung des Christentums', *Beijing Rundschau*, XXVI/12 (21 March 1989), p. 23.

142. Letter of February, 1990, from Dr. Dale A. Meyer, speaker, 'The Lutheran Hour', International Lutheran Laymen's League, St. Louis, Missouri. See also David L. Miller, 'Living in Mao's Shadow: Chinese Christians Walk a Tightrope Between the Faith and the Party', *The Lutheran*, 24 1989, pp. 16–19.

143. Quoted in Howard F. Vos, *Religions in a Changing World* (Chicago: Moody Press, 1959), pp. 157–58.

144. Miller, *op. cit.*, p. 18.

145. *Chinese Theological Review* (1986), pp. 46–70; the article originally appeared in the December 1985 issue of the *Nanjing Theological Review*. The *Chinese Theological Review* contains many essays in support of the Three-Self Movement and its ideals; see, for example, in the 1986 volume, pp. 5 ff. and 18 ff.; in the 1987 number, pp. 31 ff. and 53 ff.

146. K. H. Ting, *Christian Witness in China Today* (Kyoto, Japan: Doshisha University Press, 1985), pp. 13–14, 47–48.

147. E.g., Ding Guangxun and Wang Weifan, 'Religion Opium des Volkes?', *Beijing Rundschau*, XXVI/12 (21 March 1989), pp. 16–22.

148. For reliable firsthand monitoring reports, contact the China Church Centre (Jonathan Chao), Shatin, Hong Kong.

149. Miller, *loc. cit.* The very latest news reports indicate that the situation is in fact deteriorating further: Jonathan Mirsky reports from Hong Kong in *The Times* [London], 7 February 1994: 'Peking tightens curbs on religion. China has issued regulations reinforcing its tight control of all religious activities, especially practices outside the Communist Party's officially approved "patriotic" churches, temples and mosques.

    'The restrictions, signed by Li Peng, the Prime Minister, prohibit foreigners and overseas Chinese giving funds to believers and from supplying religious materials which "threaten China's social and public order". For example, anything which suggests the supremacy of the Pope over Catholics, or of the Dalai Lama over his followers, is illegal.

    'Most of the regulations are restatements of past Chinese laws on religion, which in essence criminalise activities outside the party's control. But they point to the state's increasing anxiety over the instability of China's border areas, where Muslims and Tibetans are in perpetual ferment. These fears have been heightened by religious conflicts in Eastern Europe and the former Soviet Union.'

150. Quoted in Mueller, *op. cit.*, pp. 111–12.

151. James H. Taylor III, 'Church Alive in Mainland China', *Chinese Around the World*, September 1986, p. 4. This periodical, *Chinese Around the World*, published by the Chinese Co-ordination Centre of World Evangelism, is the very best source of current information on the challenge of China for western Christians; it will be sent free to those requesting it (CATW, P.O. Box 98435, TST, Hong Kong).

152. Eric Liddell, *The Disciplines of the Christian Life* (*op. cit.*), passim, but especially pp. 152–55. On pp. 79–81, he identifies the Kingdom of God and the Kingdom of Heaven with 'Christ's lofty vision to make a beautiful world'!

153. See Montgomery, *Faith Founded on Fact* (*op. cit.*), passim.

154. *China: An Introduction* (*op. cit.*), pp. 15–16.

155. Hajime Nakamura, *Ways of Thinking of Eastern Peoples: India-China-Tibet-Japan*, ed. Philip P. Wiener (Honolulu, Hawaii: East-West Center Press, 1964).

156. Ethel R. Nelson, 'Prologue' to *The Discovery of Genesis: How the Truths of Genesis Were Found Hidden in the Chinese*

Language, by C. H. Kang and Ethel R. Nelson (St. Louis, Missouri: Concordia Publishing House, 1979), pp. xii-xiii.

157. *Ibid.*, pp. 118-19. More recently, Dr. Nelson has provided an even more rigorous treatment of this subject by limiting her argument strictly to the most ancient forms of Chinese writing ('Bronze-ware' and 'Oracle Bone'): Ethel R. Nelson and Richard E. Broadberry, *Mysteries Confucius Couldn't Solve: Analyses of Ancient Characters Reveal Intriguing Facts Shared with Hebrew Scriptures* (Dunlap, Tennessee: Read Books, 1986). The same work is published in Chinese by Living Stone Press, P.O. Box 17, 160 Taipei, Taiwan.

158. Nakamura, *op. cit.*, p. 16.

159. *Cf.* the classic novel *The Scholars* by Wu Ching-tzu (3d ed. Beijing: Foreign Languages Press, 1973).

160. My presentation on that occasion (having nothing to do with Eastern religions, but with Sherlock Holmes' apologetics) is included in Montgomery, *The Transcendent Holmes* (Ashcroft, British Columbia: Calabash Press, 2000).

161. *Cf. Paul Tillich and Asian Religions*, ed. Ka-fu Keith Chan and Yau-nang William Ng (Berlin: De Gruyter, 2017).

162. Scott London, 'The Future of Religion: An Interview with Ninian Smart', https://scott.london/interviews/smart.html.

163. Montgomery, *Wohin marschiert China?* (Neuhausen-Stuttgart: Haenssler, 1991); *Giant in Chains: Today and Tomorrow* (Milton Keynes, England: Nelson Word, 1994). We suggest that the reader go to part 1 for a more detailed discussion of Confucian and Taoist ideologies and the Chinese religious situation in general.

164. John 14:6: 'I [Jesus] am the way, the truth, and the life: no one cometh unto the Father, but by me.' Acts 4:12 (the original apostolic preaching): 'Neither is there salvation in any other: for there is none other name [than that of Jesus] under heaven given among men, whereby we must be saved.'

165. Barbara Aria, *The Spirit of the Chinese Character* (San Francisco: Chronicle Books, 1992). Sadly, the book does not employ the now standard Pinyin transcriptions of Hanzi characters, and traditional and simplified characters are interspersed without identification as to which are being employed.

166. Note the difference in tonality as compared with 'ritual' (*lǐ*)— our note 10, *infra*.

167. *Cf.* Montgomery, 'Evangelical Chauvinism', in his *Defending the Gospel in Legal Style* (Bonn, Germany: Verlag fuer Kultur und Wissenschaft, 2017).

168. See especially *Xunzi: The Complete Text*, trans. and ed. Eric L. Hutton (Princeton, New Jersey: Princeton University Press, 2014).

169. The concept of *ritual* (literary character 禮, *lǐ*) is nowhere carefully defined; it refers in the Confucian philosophical tradition to products of scholarly/sage thinking and practise across the Chinese centuries. For a Western parallel, think of the Roman Catholic employment of the notion of 'tradition' (with or without capitalization). The problem, in all such cases, is to discover what is the *true* tradition or ritual, as compared to what is offered by false teachers or by accretions inconsistent with the fundamental truths of the given value system.

170. *Ibid.*, p. 248.

171. As a youthful Scout (an *Eagle* Scout *with silver palms*, NB), I reverently recited both. The last few years have seen devastating lawsuits against the Boy Scouts of America for condoning the sexual corruption and maltreatment of a not inconsiderable number of their young members.

172. Michael Licona, *The Resurrection of Jesus: A New Historiographical Approach* (Downers Grove, Illinois: IVP Academic, 2010), p. 34.

173. *Ibid.*, p. 593.

174. James W. Voelz and Christopher W. Mitchell, *Mark 8:27–16:20* (Concordia Commentary; St. Louis: Concordia Publishing House, 2019), p. 597.

175. Dr. Voelz has claimed that my critique of his position is unfounded. Here is my reply:

    Pace, I have read Dr. Voelz' work carefully, and I stand by what I have written.

    1. When Dr. Voelz says that 'the story of Jesus is *true* in a way that the Odysseus tale is not', the key question is, 'true' *in what way?* Of course, the Jesus narrative is 'a better story'. But is it, *in all its details, a reliable historical*

record of what in fact occurred? And is this the case for the entire Gospel of Mark—and the rest of biblical revelation, for that matter?

2. Dr. Voelz does indeed assert that the Near Eastern myths such as the Odysseus story 'provided a *cultural preparation* for the true expression of the interaction between God and man, namely, that which has occurred in the person of Jesus Christ'. But, to be sure, the issue is the meaning of 'true expression' and 'that which has occurred'. These phrases have been employed for years in New Testament scholarship without any necessary reference to *historical truth*. When I taught at a Lutheran theological seminary in California, a distinguished New Testament scholar at the Church Divinity School of the Pacific spoke in much the same terms as Dr. Voelz: the story of Jesus was indeed of the highest truth—metaphysically, literarily; but its saving power did not depend on its literal, historical facticity. One thinks of Bishop James Pike's well-known affirmation that he could 'sing the Creed but not say it'—meaning that he believed it 'true' (personally, existentially) but not necessarily as factual history.

3. Christian littérateurs such as J. R. R. Tolkien and C. S. Lewis have made the point better than Dr. Voelz that the myths of antiquity function as a *preparatio evangelica*. But, in doing so, they leave no doubt that the real superiority of the Jesus story lies in its historical veracity (see my book, *Myth, Allegory and Gospel*). If Dr. Voelz believes himself misunderstood, why does he not eliminate all ambiguity by affirming the *de facto historicity* of the biblical events on which he is commenting?

176. *Cf.* Kenneth M. Sroka, 'The Function of Form: Ivanhoe As Romance', *Studies in English Literature* (Rice University), 19/4 [Autumn, 1979], pp. 645–61.

177. In the little office to which he had been relegated, de Gaulle said to an incredulous René Cassin, 'Cassin, we *are* France.'

178. Churchill's remark is well-known: 'My hardest cross to bear was the Cross of Lorraine.'

179. J. Barton Payne, 'Hermeneutics as a Cloak for the Denial of Scripture', *Bulletin of the Evangelical. Theological Society* 3/4 (Fall 1960), pp. 93–100.

180. Jean-Marie Schaeffer, 'Fictional vs. Factual Narration', *Living Handbook of Narratology*, sec. 3:3, http://www.lhn.uni-hamburg.de/node/56.html *Cf.* also Schaeffer's *Pourquoi la fiction?* (Paris: Le Seuil, 1999), also in English translation.

181. A particularly egregious example is Michael Licona. See the previous chapter of this volume and Lydia McGrew, *The Mirror or the Mask: Liberating the Gospels from Literary Devices* (Tampa, Florida: DeWard, 2019).

182. *Cf.* H. C. Chang, *Tales of the Supernatural*, Chinese Literature 3 (Edinburgh: Edinburgh University Press, 1983).

183. English translation in *The Man Who Sold a Ghost*, trans. Yang Hsien-Yi and Gladys Yang (2nd ed.; Peking: Foreign Languages Press, 1990), pp. 112–13.

184. See Montgomery, *Tractatus Logico-Theologicus* (6th ed.; Bonn, Germany: Verlag fuer Kultur und Wissenschaft, 2019), sec. 3.67.

185. Lu Hsun/Xun, *A Brief History of Chinese Fiction*, trans. Yang Hsien-Yi and Gladys Yang (3rd ed.; Peking: Foreign Languages Press, 1976), sec. 5 ('Tales of the Supernatural in the Six Dynasties').

186. See, *inter alia*, Montgomery, *History, Law, and Christianity* (3rd ed.; Irvine, California: New Reformation Press, 2015).

187. This evidence is summarised in Richard Bauckham's *Jesus and the Eyewitnesses: The Gospels as Eyewitness Testimony* (2nd ed.; Grand Rapids, Michigan: Eerdmans, 2017), p. 84.

188. Now largely supplanted by Pinyin romanisation. *Cf.* Raymong Chang and Margareyt Scrogin Chang, *Speaking of Chinese* (rev. ed.; London: André Deutsch, 1980).

189. *Strange Stories from a Chinese Studio*, trans. Herbert. A. Giles (rev. 3rd ed.; Shanghai: Kelly & Walsh, 1916).

190. John Minford and Tong Man, 'Whose Strange Stories? P'u Sung-ling (1640–1715), Herbert Giles (1845–1935), and the *Liao-chai chih-yi*', *East Asian History*, 17/18 (June/December, 1999), p. 1.

191. Herbert Allen Giles, *Chinese Sketches* (London: Trübner, 1876), pp. 95–100.

192. 'An "old Chinese admirer" described Giles as "of the fanatical type, always furiously taking sides no matter right or wrong." Minford and Tong, *op. cit.*, p. 2.

193. Giles, *Chinese Sketches*, pp. 98–99.

194. 'The Memoirs of H. A. Giles', ed. Charles Aylmer, *East Asian History*, 13/14 (June/December 1997), pp. 1–90.

195. *Ibid.*, pp. 1–2.

196. *Foreign Quarterly Review* (Treuttel, 1854), p. 552. H. A. Giles' father's negative judgement against the primary-source historicity of the Gospel records is thoroughly contradicted by the best modern scholarship; see, e.g., Bauckham, *Jesus and the Eyewitnesses*.

197. No relation to President Jack and Professor Robert Preus of the Lutheran Church–Missouri Synod.

198. Roland F. Ziegler, 'Eduard Preuss and C. F. W. Walther', *Concordia Theological Quarterly*, LXXV/3/4 (July/October 2011), pp. 289–310.

199. In our own time, one thinks of the treatment Southern Baptist seminary president Paige Patterson and Lutherans Dr. Robert Preus and the Rev. Herman Otten received at the hands of their denominations.

200. Now available, in revised edition, from New Reformation Press / 1517: The Legacy Project.

201. For reliable press reports, see the *Washington Post*, the *Wall Street Journal*, the *South China Morning Post*, etc. The 24–25 April 2020 edition of *Figaro Magazine* features as its cover story 'Le grand déni chinois' (The big Chinese denial), arguing that the totalitarian, Marxist government of China has 'never told the truth' as to 'the emergence, the extent, and the statistics of the pandemic'. This lead article is followed by another titled (my translation) 'Seventy Years of Lying/Deception/Falsehoods in Communist China'.

202. Vivien Sung, *Bonheur, bonheurs*, Chinese text by You Shan Tang (San Francisco, California: Seuil Chronicle Books, 2002), pp. 31–35.

203. Jeffrey A. Cobble, 'The Coronavirus Pandemic vs. the Limits of Governmental Power', Cobble Law Firm, 2 April 2020, MS Word document, https://tntrafficticket.us/wp-content/uploads/2020/05/V-19-vs.-Limits-of-Governmental-Power.doc.

204. The quoted material appears in boldface in the original web article.

205. Jeannie Thomas Parker, *The Mythic Chinese Unicorn*, accessed 8 March 2021, http://chinese-unicorn.com/ch01/. This detailed treatment is unfortunately available only as a web edition.

206. The Unicorn of Justice pictured here is one of the Chinese mythological figurines in the Montgomery collection.

207. See, in particular, *Wildfire Policy: Law and Economics Perspectives*, ed. Dean Lueck and Karen M. Bradshaw (London: Routledge, 2013).

208. *Bl. Com.* IV, xiv, 3. See Montgomery, 'Whose Life Anyway? A Re-examination of Suicide and Assisted Suicide', in his *Christ Our Advocate* (Bonn, Germany: Verlag fuer Kultur und Wissenschaft, 2002), pp. 169–95.

209. *Strange Stories from a Chinese Studio*, trans. H. A. Giles (rev. 3rd ed.; Shanghai: Kelly & Walsh, 1916), p. 261.

210. John Piper, "How God Visits Sins on the Third and Fourth Generation," desiringGod, 6 March 2009, https://www.desiringgod.org/articles/how-god-visits-sins-on-the-third-and-fourth-generation (Piper's italics).

THE AUTHOR

JOHN WARWICK MONTGOMERY is considered by many to be the foremost living apologist for biblical Christianity. A renaissance scholar with a flair for controversy, he lives in France, England and the United States. His international activities have brought him into personal contact with some of the most exciting events of our time; not only was he in China in June 1989, but he was in Fiji during its 1987 bloodless revolution, was involved in assisting East Germans to escape during the time of the Berlin Wall, and was in Paris during the "days of May" 1968.

Dr. Montgomery is the author or editor of more than sixty books in six languages. He holds eleven earned degrees, including a Master of Philosophy in Law from the University of Essex, England, an LL.M. and the earned higher doctorate in law (LL.D.) from Cardiff University, Wales, a Ph.D. from the University of Chicago, and a Doctorate of the University in Protestant Theology from the University of Strasbourg, France, as well as the higher doctorate in law (LL.D.) from Cardiff University, Wales, U.K. He is an ordained Lutheran clergyman, an English barrister, a French *avocat* (barreau de Paris), and is admitted to practice as a lawyer before the Supreme Court of the United States. He obtained acquittals for the "Athens 3" missionaries on charges of proselytism at the Greek Court of Appeals in 1986, and has won four religious cases at the European Court of Human Rights.

After receiving emeritus status as Professor of Law and Humanities at the University of Bedfordshire, England, Dr. Montgomery has been serving as Professor-at-Large for 1517 (www.1517.org), Irvine, California. He annually conducts the residential programme of the International Academy of Apologetics, Evangelism, and Human Rights in Strasbourg, France. Recently, he earned a Diploma in Basic Chinese Language Studies (Alison, Ireland, in conjunction with Cambridge University). Biographical articles on him appear in *Who's Who in America*, *Who's Who in France*, *Who's Who in Europe*, and *Who's Who in the World*.

INDEX OF NAMES

Andropov, 159
Aquinas, Thomas, 65, 145
Aria, Barbara, 182
Aristotle, 107, 191
Armstrong, William, 32
Aspinall, John, 207
Augustine (St.), 143

Bach, J. S., 72
Baier, Kurt, 137, 138
Bao Jia-quan (Pastor), 14
Beria, 42
Bian Hanwu, 36
Blackstone, William, 214
Buchsel, Karl, 202
Buckley, William F., 32
Buddha, 119, 120, 129, 130, 131
Burkhardt, 98, 101, 113
Bush, George, 31, 32, 38, 52, 53, 60, 61

Caesar Augustus, 195
Callaway, 130
Catlin, George, 65
Ceausescu, Nicolae, 54, 55, 63
Chalidze, 77
Chamberlain, 96, 97
Chambers, Oswald, 152
Ch'ang-tzu, 107
Chardin, Teilhard de, 162

Chen, 72
Chen Xitong, 6
Chiang Kai-shek, 153, 154
Condillac, 6
Confucius, 105, 110, 112, 113, 114, 115, 116, 117, 182, 183, 184, 185, 187, 200

de Gaulle, Charles, 191
Deng Liqun, 49
Deng Xiaoping, 6, 11, 29, 32, 37, 41, 42, 51, 57, 61, 62, 63, 85, 91, 103, 135, 177
Ding Shisun, 44
Donne, John, 112, 215
Dumas, Roland, 29

Elert, Werner, 144
Engels, 65, 66, 67, 68, 80

Fairbank, John King, 93
Fang Ke, 6
Fang Lizhi, 6
Fosdick, Harry Emerson, 171
Frisbie, John, 59
Fujioka, 130

Gandhi, 26
Gates, Alan F., 157
Gautama, 119, 120

Gejdenson, Sam, 53
Gerhard, Johann, 203
Giles, Herbert Allen, 199, 200, 201, 202, 217
Giles, John Allen, 201
Glasser, 157
Gorbachev, ix, 5, 65, 71, 85, 86, 89, 90, 91
Goude, Jean Paul, 30
Graham, Billy, 14

Hauck, 143
He Dongchang, 44
Hegel, 74, 75, 79, 81
He Jingzhi, 48, 49
Herod, 196
Herzog, 143
Hesse, I., 106
Hick, John, 181
Higgins, Jack, 76
Hitler, 29, 30
Hobbes, 66
Homer, 190
Hsun Tzu, 114
Hugo, Victor, 11
Hume, 107, 132
Hu Yaobang, 4, 9, 56

Innocent III (Pope), 160

Jiang Qing, 80
Jiang Zemin, 6, 57, 62
John, Griffith, 147
John the Baptist, 196
John the Constant, 203
Jones, E. Stanley, 171

Kang (Pastor), 173, 174
Kant, 113, 114
Kaptchuk, 109
Kawasaki, Kenryo, 130
Koestler, Arthur, 132, 133
Kublai Khan, 142

Lao-tze, 105, 106, 110, 111, 182
Lasswell, 72
Latourette, Kenneth Scott, 100, 101, 103, 133, 145
Legge, James, 117
Lei Feng, 26
Lenin, 55, 81, 87, 89
Lewis, C. S., 106
Liang Xiang, 47
Licona, Michael, 189
Liddell, Eric, 154, 155, 171
Lin Biao, 80
Lindsell, Harold, 169
Li Peng, 5, 26, 27, 28, 30, 57
Li Po, v
Löwith, Karl, 74
Luke, 196
Luther, Martin, 144, 162

MacArthur, Douglas, 211
Machiavelli, 113
MacInnes, Peter, 16
Mao Tse-tung, 8, 37, 41, 57, 80, 81, 92, 104, 154, 157, 158, 159
Mark, 190
Marx, 63, 65, 66, 67, 68, 69, 70, 72, 73, 74, 75, 80, 89
Masutani Fumio, 129
McDougal, 72
McGrew, Lydia, 189, 190
Mencius, 112, 113, 185, 187
Merton, Thomas, 12
Miller, 168
Milton, 73
Ming Ti, 106
Moody, Dwight, 149, 150, 151
Morrison, Robert, 143, 145, 148
Munro, 117
Murphy, Cornelius, 78

Nakamura, 176
Nebuchadnezzar, 91

Index of Names 243

Needham, 108
Nestorius, 141
Nixon, Richard, 63
Noah, 173

Okamoto, Kanei, 130
Orwell, George, 18, 39, 73

Paley, 202
Partsch, Karl Josef, 30
Paul (St.), 170
Pharaoh, 91
Phillips, D. Z., 181
Piper, John, 217
Plato, 114
Polo, Marco, 141, 142
Pontius Pilate, 195
Preuss, Eduard, 202, 203, 204
Pu Songling, 199

Qian Liren, 43
Qin Shi Huang, 12

Ricci, Matteo, 142, 143

Santayana, George, 192
Saul (King), 139
Schaeffer, Jean-Marie, 192
Schroeder, Gary (Pastor), 25
Scott, Walter, 191
Scowcroft, Brent, 52, 58
Sma Chien, 105
Smart, Ninian, 181
Smith, G. W., 75
Smith, Stanley P., 150
Solzhenitsyn, 120
Sparks, 120
Steinilber-Oberlin, 129
Stock, Eugene, 151
Studd, Charles T., 150
Studd, J. E. K., 151

Sun (Pastor), 12
Sun Yat-sen, 93, 153, 166

Tamarlane, 142
Tan Wenrui, 43
Taylor, Hudson James, 148, 149, 151, 168
Taylor, James H., III, 169, 170, 172
Tian Jing-fu, 12
Tillich, Paul, 181
Ting, K. H., 165
Tolkien, J. R. R., 191
Toynbee, Arnold, ix
Tso Tsung-te, 147

Uerkesh, Daolet, 5, 6

Voegelin, Eric, 76
Voelz, James, 189, 190, 199

Wang Dan, 6
Wang Meng, 47, 48
Wang Ming Tao, 161, 162
Wan Li, 6
Warfield, B. B., 192
Warneck, Gustav, 143, 144
Wittgenstein, Ludwig, 137, 138
Wu Shuqing, 44

Xu Guoming, 36

Yang, C. K., 104
Yang, Y. C., 112, 114, 117, 132
Yang Shankun, 5
Yan Jiaqi, 50
Yan Xuerong, 36

Zhao Ziyang, 5, 6, 28, 47, 50, 62
Zheng Tuobin, 38
Zhou Enlai, 26
Ziegler, Roland F., 202

www.ingramcontent.com/pod-product-compliance
Lightning Source LLC
LaVergne TN
LVHW041331080426
835512LV00006B/405